Lessons from Tara

Lessons from Tara

Life Advice
from the World's
Most Brilliant Dog

David Rosenfelt

sphere

SPHERE

First published in Great Britain in 2015 by Sphere
This paperback edition published in 2016 by Sphere

1 3 5 7 9 10 8 6 4 2

A CIP catalogue record for this book
is available from the British Library.

ISBN 978-0-7515-6367-2

Printed and bound in Great Britain by
Clays Ltd, St Ives plc

Papers used by Sphere are from well-managed forests
and other responsible sources.

MIX
Paper from
responsible sources
FSC® C104740

Sphere
An imprint of
Little, Brown Book Group
Carmelite House
50 Victoria Embankment
London EC4Y 0DZ

An Hachette UK Company
www.hachette.co.uk

www.littlebrown.co.uk

This book is dedicated to the many wonderful friends we have met here in Maine.

Lessons from Tara

It can all be traced to Tara. . . .

The whole thing, all that my wife, Debbie Myers, and I did and are doing: The decision to get involved in rescue, volunteering in awful Southern California shelters, starting our own foundation, rescuing four thousand dogs, putting in those endless hours, adopting an absolutely ridiculous lifestyle, and becoming certified dog lunatics.

If not for Tara we never would have had a house filled with dogs these last two decades . . . never less than twenty, and a high of forty-two. I wouldn't have included a dog rescue theme in my Andy Carpenter books, and there's no doubt that a lot fewer people would have read them. I certainly would never have lived through, nor written, *Dogtripping.*

Our house wouldn't always be knee-deep in dog hair, and we wouldn't go through vacuum cleaners every six months. I wouldn't have taken my laser printer in to be fixed, only to have the guy tell me that there was enough hair stuck in it to make a coat. I wouldn't be literally shoveling shit every morning, and I might not have had four back surgeries. We would be using plastic grocery bags to carry groceries, and not for . . . other purposes.

We wouldn't have made a succession of veterinarians wealthy, there wouldn't be a mastiff and four other dogs sleeping in our bed every night, and my car, the one we use for shuttling dogs around, wouldn't be affectionately and accurately dubbed, "The Shit-mobile." There wouldn't be a layer of dog hair on every piece of clothing I own.

Debbie Myers and I might have only dated a couple of times, and thus never fallen in love. I never would have become aware of the amazing love and comfort that dogs have to offer, and how worth it it is to deal with the pain of losing one . . and then another . . . and then another. I certainly wouldn't be getting my face licked on a regular basis.

I wouldn't go though a couple hundred pounds of kibble a week, or dispense more medication than the average Rite Aid. It wouldn't take me almost an hour to give out upwards of sixty pills a day. The local PetSmart employees wouldn't spread rose petals in front of me when I arrive at their store, or know exactly what I want without my having to ask for it.

Strangers wouldn't want to visit our house, considering it sort of a canine Disneyland. Our FedEx driver wouldn't tell me that he has other customers in nearby towns who ask him if he knows where we live. People I meet for the first time wouldn't eventually snap their fingers and say, "Wait a minute . . . are you that dog guy?" In fact, I wouldn't actually be "that dog guy."

I wouldn't get up at five thirty every morning to the sound of barking, nor would I cringe every time a doorbell rings in a television commercial. Halloween wouldn't be the most dreaded night of the year. I wouldn't have to navigate a canine minefield to go to the bathroom in the middle of the night. And I wouldn't hear more retching noises during the night than you'd hear in the average fraternity house after an all-night party. "Watch your step" would not be words to live by.

I wouldn't have had a chance to get to know dog rescuers all over the country, and if there is a more dedicated, greater group of people anywhere, I'd sure like to meet them. I never would have realized that there was a massive subculture of dog lovers that exists anywhere you could go. And I would not have been able to help any of them raise money for their very worthy causes.

There would be less screaming in our house, less vacuuming, less mopping, more sleeping, more relaxing, and much less love.

So Tara changed my life and taught me more than I would have thought possible. Some of it was through her actions, but most of it was through her legacy, and the descendants she left behind. They literally number in the thousands.

The lessons in this book are the ones I learned from Tara and her friends. She never met any of them, but she saved every one of their lives.

And I am forever grateful.

Tara taught me . . .

in bed, it's best to be on the bottom.

G et your mind out of the gutter; this is not that kind of book.

Tara used to sleep in bed with Debbie and me, but she would always arrive late. I'm not sure why; it's not like she was returning from a night out clubbing. It was just part of her routine to sleep on the living room couch, then get up and come sauntering into the bedroom at around two in the morning. She'd then climb up and go to sleep. It really wasn't a problem for her, since she didn't have to get up and go to work in the morning.

We had a California king bed, so there was plenty of room, but Tara didn't necessarily see it that way. Rather than look for an available slot, she would lie on top of either Debbie's or my legs. It was actually a comforting feeling, and I was always pleased when she chose me, though it was fairly rare that she did.

Fast forward to now, and there are always at least four dogs on the bed, though it can be as many as six. The regulars are Wanda, the mastiff; Jenny, a lab mix; Cheyenne, a Great Pyrenees; and Boomer, Cheyenne's sister. And these are not small dogs; they represent a little more than four hundred pounds of dog. We still have a California king—because we can't find anything larger.

At four A.M., so regular that you can set your watch by it, Bernie the Bernese mountain dog starts to bark, softly at first, then louder. While barking, he puts his front paws on the bed, a signal that we are supposed to lift him up.

He could make it up there himself, but somehow seems to consider it beneath his dignity to do so. Debbie and I both pretend not to hear him, until one of us (usually me) gives up and hoists all 120 pounds of him onto the bed.

The act of lifting him is more than just a question of strength and effort. It's also a strategic challenge, because the other dogs sometimes have to be repositioned so as to find a space on which to hoist him. They are all asleep, and would not react well to a Bernese mountain dog landing on them. They are not as tolerant as Debbie and I.

Once I've successfully added Bernie's very large frame to the crowd, I've got another challenge. Except for Jenny, who shares my pillow, and Cheyenne, who insists on resting her head on a human's upper torso, the rest of them like to sleep near the other end of the bed, blocking off half of it.

That leaves me three choices. One would be to lie in the fetal position, knees up near my chin. That would be fine, unless I wanted to stretch out, or fall asleep, or be able to walk in the morning. The fetal position works fine for fetuses, because they get to stay in one place, and don't have to lift forty-pound bags of kibble.

The second option would be to rest my feet on top of one or more of the dogs, in effect turning them into canine ottomans. That might actually be fairly comfortable, until one of them decided they wanted to get up. If Wanda the mastiff was the one to make that decision, I would immediately feel like I was going into traction, and real traction would soon follow.

The third, Tara-inspired choice, is the perfect option. I burrow my feet under them. They don't seem to mind, I'm able to stretch out, and I get that comforting feeling of them lying across my legs. Of course, when it's the 175-pound Wanda, or even Bernie, it feels like my legs are propping up South Dakota. But it still works fine, and it is particularly warming on cold Maine winter nights. Wanda has so much padding, I don't even think she notices.

Of course, even this has its drawbacks. For one thing, rolling over becomes an impossibility, at least for the lower half of my body. And if one of my "foot blankets" should happen to drool, it would provoke an unpleasant, even disgusting, sensation.

In addition to our bed not being the most comfortable of places, it's not the most sanitary of environments either, since dogs have a tendency to shed as well as drool where they sleep. The trick is for us to pretend we're out camping, and think of it all as communing with nature.

One night, when Debbie was out of town, I got into bed, initially joined by three dogs. The television is on the wall to the left, so I was looking in that direction, watching it. The lights were off in the room, but the television has a very large screen, and it was providing a substantial bit of illumination. I don't remember what was on, but there's close to a one hundred percent chance it was a sporting event of some kind.

Suddenly, from the television side of the bed, Wanda appeared. She is so large that she doesn't jump on the bed, she walks up on it. And that was what she was doing, slowly and deliberately. Wanda doesn't scamper or dart, she plods. She gets where she is going, not quickly, but eventually.

In a few seconds she was standing on the bed, her massive frame coming toward me, the television behind her. What I noticed immediately was the large amount of drool dripping from each side of her mouth.

This in itself was not exactly a shocking event; Wanda is a walking saliva factory. I generally don't mind the fact that she drools; my problem is how she gets rid of it. She doesn't dab it away with a napkin, but rather shakes her head from side to side, spraying it everywhere.

But on this particular night the drool was much more than normal, and I don't know what was causing it. Perhaps she had just finished eating a tree, or maybe a car. I didn't have time to reflect on the cause of her drool, because she was heading in my direction. She was eerily backlit by the television, which made it look like neon drool.

She came toward me, towering, slowly and ponderously. Had Godzilla moved that slowly toward the city of Tokyo, the panicked citizens could have had a few beers, taken in a movie, and then casually ambled away. It felt like it took ten minutes, but it was really only a few seconds. I couldn't take my eyes off the sparkling drool, but I knew where it was headed.

My pillow.

Wanda plunked her massive head next to me on the pillow, and the body followed with a thud. The entire episode was disgusting, so I did what Debbie and I have learned to do in these situations.

I turned my side of the pillow over, closed my eyes, and went to sleep, right next to the Great Wall of Wanda. The drool would be dry by morning, and I wanted to get to sleep before she started snoring. Her snoring sounds like a road crew drilling into concrete.

Of course there are other challenges to sleeping in our house that Tara did not teach me how to deal with, like the unbelievable noise, and I don't just mean Wanda's snoring. Tara was comparatively quiet, only barking when there was a reason to, and even then not very loudly. Such is not the case in our house now.

When I lived in New York, I used to pride myself on being a city guy, able to deal with the difficulties that urban life presented. For instance, at night there were frequent noises, such as car horns, early morning garbage trucks, drive-by shootings, car bombs . . . that kind of stuff. Sounds of the city.

But when you're a New York guy like me, you learn to adjust. You get used to the noise, and you either sleep through it, or you go to the window and yell profanities at the people making the racket. When they're finished yelling back at you and saying horrible things about your mother, you fall back to sleep without much of a problem. That's what us tough city guys do; we accept it as part of the natural order of things.

That was then; this is now. I challenge any city guy to come sleep for a night in our shoes, much less our bed. Compared to what we deal with every night, spending a night in Manhattan is like sleeping in the cone of silence.

I would say there are five or six outbursts of barking every night. I have no idea why; maybe the dogs sense something outside, or maybe they're just deliberately being obnoxious. But imagine a police car driving through your bedroom, sirens blaring, and with the cops firing their weapons out the window. That's the level of sound we're dealing with. There is no hearing person on the planet who could sleep soundly through it.

The cause of at least three outbursts a night is Ralph, a black lab who camps himself on the landing at the top of the stairs leading to our bedroom. He's like the bouncer outside the bar, checking IDs and hand stamps. Late-arriving dogs are afraid to walk by Ralph, who growls at them. But they want to get into the bedroom so they stand on the steps and bark at Ralph, in effect telling him to move.

Ralph has no interest in moving, and, unlike Debbie and I, is really not put off at all by late-night barking. But the dogs wanting to get by are apparently optimists, and believe that if they continue to bark as loudly as they can, Ralph will see the light and get the hell out of the way.

Of course he doesn't, so in each case I have to get up and escort the barking dog past Ralph and into the bedroom. Then Ralph goes back to sleep and waits for the next trespasser, so the entire process can be repeated. I have tried moving Ralph to comfortable dog beds or pieces of furniture, but he prefers the top of the stairs, and the feeling of power it gives him.

If it was just the barking, the nights would be almost bearable, emphasis on the "almost." But there are all kinds of other noises. Growling, scratching, wrestling, snoring . . . they all have their distinctive sounds. It's like sleeping in the jungle, but with a television and running water.

Probably the worst noisemaker is a senior golden retriever named Mamie, who makes a retching sound that sounds like she's throwing up a lung two or three times a night. It's a dry heave; nothing actually comes out (or if it does, it's happily gone by morning). She's been doing it for years, and has been checked by a vet on numerous occasions. There is no obvious physical reason for it; it's just part of her charm.

As you might guess, lack of sleep leaves me tired a lot, so I attempt to take some daytime naps. As I mentioned, our bedroom is upstairs, and once I put one foot on the steps, my "nap team" springs into action. Benji, Cody, Wanda, Molly, Jenny, and Otis all share the bed with me while I'm napping, and they run up ahead of me and get into position before I even arrive.

I rarely go upstairs during the day unless I'm going to take a nap, and I try not to do so. I feel guilty that my nap team is so disappointed if I get up there and don't climb into bed.

Debbie has an almost entirely different nap team; only Wanda and Molly overlap with mine. So, of course, we can't take naps together; there simply isn't room for both teams. I have no idea why the different nap teams are structured this way, or why certain dogs want to be on the bed during daytime naps, but not nighttime sleep. Maybe they've just divvied us up among themselves.

But, like everything else about our house, it's bizarre and exhausting.

Tara taught me . . .

about dating and women.

B ack in the days when I was single, it is fair to say that I
did not live a bachelor's dream life. To those of you who
have met me, this probably does not come as a big surprise.

Were I to stand on a phone book, in the event that phone
books still existed, I would be six feet tall. I don't want to be
too self-critical, but my distinguishing physical feature has always been my nondescriptness. If I were to set a low bar for
success, I would say that girls, and then women, never seemed
to recoil from me.

And then I met Debbie Myers, who introduced me to her
golden retriever, the aforementioned Tara. We started to
date, and many of those dates included Tara. We took her on
walks, to beaches, outdoor restaurants, etc. I will admit to
having been head over heels for both of them.

Debbie was a senior vice president for the Fox Network in those days, and she worked in an office all day. So I offered to drive up to her house once or twice a day and take Tara for walks. It was an offer both she and Tara happily accepted.

I did it because walking with Tara was a hell of a lot more appealing than sitting in my own house, waiting for a movie or television executive to call and hire me to write a script. Since those calls pretty much never came, and since Tara was always wagging her tail eagerly at the prospect of walking, the decision to do it was basically a no-brainer.

But I received an added bonus; Debbie found it very appealing. At first I assumed it was just that she was grateful I was doing her this favor, and also providing Tara with the walks that she loved. But that turned out not to be the main factor at all. It was my attitude toward Tara that provoked the positive reaction; she liked me because I liked her dog!

And even more amazingly, she wasn't the only one. When I was hanging out alone with Tara, maybe outdoors at a Starbucks, women would come up to me . . . to us.

And they would talk!

Yes, the comments were canine in nature. "Can I pet your dog?" "Oh, she's so cute." "How old is she?" "Where did you get her?" Not exactly Algonquin Roundtable conversation, but that is not even close to the point. These were women approaching me, unsolicited, and speaking. Out loud. And smiling while they did it.

This was not the natural order of things.

Now you would be correct in assuming that I was not interested in dating these women, because I was quite happy with Debbie. And yes, even I would not be slimeball enough to use one woman's dog to attract someone else. All right, I might, but not in this case. Tara was so smart she probably would have squealed on me.

But please focus on the big picture here. I was being presented with a key to a world I had heretofore never inhabited. I mean, the only thing I ever picked up in a bar was a drink, and occasionally a cold. Now, suddenly, things were different, and even though I had no desire to take advantage of that difference, the very significant point is that I could have.

Then, a couple of years later, I made a discovery that dwarfed this revelation. Having and caring for a dog is one thing; caring for and protecting a rescue dog is an entirely different ball game.

I don't pretend to completely understand why, but women absolutely love guys who rescue dogs. I'd better be careful that I'm not overstating this. I don't mean the average woman is going to overlook all other traits, like maybe the guy is a serial killer. But if all else is equal, telling a woman that you rescued this cute dog from death row is a romantic slam dunk.

I would go to mobile adoptions and sit there with a rescue dog, and the times the coffeehouse scenario occurred would quadruple. In the old days, friends used to tell me that I would be unable to score in a woman's house of detention with a fistful of pardons. But I'm telling you, in this new situation I had been given the key to the dating city. I could have played the rescue card at these mobile adoptions and gotten all the dates I wanted.

Too bad I didn't want any.

Alas, none of this is going to benefit me. I'm happily married to a wonderful person, and I'm 130 years old. So my dating boat, as they say, has sailed. There is as much chance I am going to pick up a woman as there is I'm going to ride a

Kentucky Derby winner. And you can throw in the Preakness, Belmont, and Breeders' Cup.

So I am offering this advice as a gift to the four or five young, single men who might read this book.

Rescue some dogs.

They don't even have to be cute; women seem to think that rescuing homely dogs is in some manner even more appealing. They also don't have to be small, or large, or pedigree, or anything. None of that matters at all.

Once you've done it, sit with the dog outside a coffeehouse or on a park bench. Feed it a bagel. Pet it a lot. Talk to it. Give it a hug. And then sit back and wait for the onslaught.

If you go four lattes without getting a date, you must be a serial killer.

Tara taught me . . .

to cry.

I don't mean she literally showed me how to cry; that came naturally to me. According to pretty much all members of my family, I bawled every time I didn't get my way until I was in college.

And I don't mean openly; I would rather set fire to myself than start sobbing in public.

And I don't mean frequently; you won't catch me sniffling at Budweiser Super Bowl commercials, or *Steel Magnolias*. I generally think that the word "tearjerker" is a description of the people who watch those movies and cry. (A notable exception to this rule was when Jim Brown got shot in *The Dirty Dozen*.)

First, I probably should explain my definition of crying. I consider myself to be crying if I have a painful lump in my throat, and an inability to talk normally without it being obvious that something is going on. I know it's a pretty low bar to set, but that's my standard, and I'm sticking to it.

If instead you go by the normally accepted definition and think crying includes tears, I can only recall one time in my adult life that I cried openly, in front of someone, and that was when Tara died. Moments after the vet gently ended her suffering and our collective three-month ordeal, Debbie and I went to Zuma Beach in Malibu. I won't say that was Tara's favorite beach; give her sand and ocean and sun, and she was at home anywhere. But it's the one we took her to most often, and it seemed like the place we wanted to be when she was gone.

I cried that day. Certainly not as much as Debbie; in the long history of crying, no one has ever cried as much as Debbie that day. But I let myself go, just a little, and probably would have felt better if I'd gone further.

But that day and, more important, the three months that Tara lived after being diagnosed with nasal carcinoma, really did change me. I had never been an emotional person before that, and while I'm not exactly a sensitive explorer of my feelings now, there's a discernible difference that I can trace back to her.

During my time with Tara, and especially those last three months, she was incredibly loving, and loyal, and sensitive, and stoic. At the end I hated what she was going through, and hated myself for not being able to make it better. And in retrospect I think we should have ended it earlier, but we were being selfish, hoping in some way that we wouldn't lose her. But that could never happen, and we should have recognized that fact.

I certainly haven't kept count, but Debbie and I have probably had to put at least three hundred dogs down, when their illnesses or old age have reduced their quality of life to an unacceptably poor level. She and I always insist on being present, to hold and pet the dog as they drift away.

I would say I have been there at least ninety percent of the time. The only time one of us is not there is when the dog is asleep during surgery, and what the vet sees during the operation tells him that the dog will never have a good quality of life. Waking the dog only to then euthanize it seems unfair, so we authorize the vet to do so while the dog is on the table.

But each time we are there, I have that painful, persistent, and annoying lump in my throat. I cover it pretty well, and I doubt the vets and their staff notice it, but Debbie certainly knows what's going on. I hate the feeling, but I seem to be stuck with it.

But that's not the worst part. Normal people are supposed to get choked up, or more, when their dog dies. That's not to say I'm normal, but I'm okay with having some of the same traits and reactions as the normals do.

What's really awful is that I now react in emotional ways to other situations as well. It's as if the floodgates have been opened, very much against my will.

A particularly painful example of this was the first in-store signing I ever did. It was at a prestigious bookstore in Brentwood, California, called Dutton's. Like many wonderful independent bookstores, it has since sadly closed.

The signing was for my first novel, *Open and Shut*, and the store management strongly suggested that I invite family and friends. They did this because they knew that if I didn't supply the people, the place would be empty. For some reason, the world had not been waiting for David Rosenfelt's debut novel.

I didn't have any family in California, and not many friends, so I glommed on to Debbie's friends, and a good crowd of at least fifty people showed up. I arrived at the store like a conquering hero, ready to sign books for the unwashed masses.

Once inside, the proprietor told me it was going to be a reading, something I hadn't expected or planned for. I was to find a four or five-page scene that the audience might enjoy. No big deal; reading my work seemed much easier than speaking extemporaneously. I looked through the early part of the book and came up with a section I thought would do fine.

The scene described the protagonist, Andy Carpenter, and his father attending a baseball game at Yankee Stadium. It's warm and funny, and their banter is easy and comfortable. Nice father-and-son stuff, until this section toward the end. Andy is talking about a play that was good for Andy's team, and bad for his father's:

"Can't even watch?" I crow. But it's more than that. In a brief, terrible instant, I realize that in fact he can't watch, can't speak, can't even sit up. He falls over and his head hits the railing in front of us, and then he slumps to the ground, his body grotesquely wedged between the seats.

And then I start screaming, screaming louder than anyone has ever screamed in Yankee Stadium. Screaming louder than anyone has ever screamed in any stadium.

But my dad can't hear me, and I'll never be eight years old again.

Halfway through the reading, I realized in my mind that I was going to get choked up when Andy's father died. I spent the next few pages silently screaming at myself, trying to get myself to think logically.

"You're an idiot! Why would you get choked up? Your father never took you to a Yankee game! He died in his sleep in Florida years ago! And you didn't get choked up when you wrote the damn scene! This is not about you!"

All to no avail. As I neared the end, I felt like I was being drawn toward the edge of a cliff, unable to stop. And sure enough, when I got to the climactic moment, my voice cracked noticeably, and I had to pause before I could finish. I was being publicly emotional about the death of a fake character that I myself made up, and I myself killed. And whose entire fake life lasted less than five pages.

It was then, and remains, among the most embarrassing moments of my life.

And ever since, if I'm teasing or torturing Debbie, as I am wont to do, she has a favorite retort. She says, calmly, "I'm very sorry . . ." then breaks into mock, sustained sobbing, and continues, "But I'm at a Yankee game, and I'm all upset!"

The bottom line is that I actually can divide my emotional life into the period before Tara, and the period after her. She taught me sensitivity, and compassion, and gave me emotional depth.

Ugh.

Tara taught me . . .

stoicism and courage.

Well, she tried to, but it just didn't take. Goldens never complain, nor do they reveal when they're not feeling well. There are ways to tell, of course. If their appetite lessens, or they're vomiting, or they don't want to interact or be playful, those are obvious signs. But it requires being alert to their actions, because they just suffer in silence.

Suffering in silence has never been my strong point, a fact that was very much in evidence in April of 2014. I woke up one morning not feeling well, which wasn't a surprise because Debbie was in the middle of a bout of bronchitis. I assumed that I was catching it, and while that would have been a bummer, it at least would have given me something to bemoan. That is when I am at my best; if there were an Olympic bemoaning team, I'd bring home the gold.

So Debbie and I swapped complaints for a short while, each of us trying to outdo the other in our professed sickness. But I really didn't have time for too much of that, because I had to drive to Southern New Hampshire. I was meeting Erika Matthews, who was with St. Hubert's Animal Shelter in New Jersey, one of the best rescue groups I have ever come across.

We were taking two senior black labs from them, because they were unable to place them in a home together. Erika was driving them to New Hampshire, and I was meeting her there. It's a routine we had done before. The round-trip would take me about five hours.

I didn't feel that terrible, and I was confident I could make the trip. I also felt an obligation, because Erika, with longer to drive than me, had already been on the road for at least an hour.

I started to feel sicker on the way, and it soon became clear that this was more than just a bout of bronchitis. By the time I got to New Hampshire, I was in pretty bad shape. I pulled up next to Erika in the parking lot where we were meeting, but instead of getting out of the car, I called her on the cell phone. I told her that I was sick, that she shouldn't get near me, and that I was going to grab the dogs out of her car and take off.

Which I did. And in about thirty seconds flat, I was back on the road home with Ralph and Randy, two absolutely adorable black labs. There was very little conversation between us on the way home; it was all I could do to drive. I kept wrestling with the idea of finding a hospital along the way, but had no idea what I would do with the dogs. Fortunately they seemed fine together, and slept peacefully most of the way.

It was the longest, most miserable car ride of my life, and there is nothing in second place.

I got home, brought the dogs into the house, staggered toward the couch, and almost made it. I collapsed onto the floor, though I think I remained conscious the entire time.

Collapsing on the floor in our house is a tricky business, and not at all recommended, because the dogs just naturally assume it's time to play. So within seconds I was covered with probably six hundred pounds of dog, all delighted by this apparent new game I was sharing with them.

Debbie insisted on calling an ambulance, but I refused to let her. She insisted again, and I refused again. After that she didn't bother discussing it with me; she just called the ambulance, and they told her they were on their way.

If you think collapsing in our house is tough, you should try getting picked up by an ambulance. Even in my very sick state, I realized that there was no way ambulance people were going to come into our house. A SWAT team would have second thoughts about coming into our house. If these particular ambulance people were smart first responders, they'd back off and wait for the second or third responders.

So I staggered out onto our front porch and lay down. Debbie came out and covered me with four blankets. It was about fifty-five degrees, but I was still shivering when the ambulance arrived, twenty minutes later. It was a really long twenty minutes.

Before too long I was in the ambulance and on the way to Miles Memorial Hospital, unaware of an unfolding chaos that I had just left behind. When I got there, they quickly examined me in the emergency room, and mentioned that I had an infection called sepsis, and was entering septic shock.

The next thing I knew I was in intensive care, the first tip-off that septic shock was not such a good thing to have. A quick Google on my iPad confirmed it; the mortality rate is forty percent.

I called Debbie, who I knew would comfort me and tell me not to worry about things at home, just to rest and get better.

As it turned out, that wasn't quite how the conversation went. Here's what she told me had happened in the two hours since the ambulance had taken me away:

1. When the ambulance left, she was so upset that she must have accidentally left the front door open.
2. The dogs ran out onto the porch, and in their excitement to chase the ambulance, crashed through and smashed the porch gate. It was beyond repair.
3. Once through the gate, they of course couldn't catch the ambulance. Our dogs are mostly old, and would be lucky to catch me. So they ran out into the neighborhood, and since we live in the middle of nowhere and our nearest neighbor is maybe a quarter mile away, that represented a complete disaster.
4. With the help of some neighbors, Ronnie and Bob Pisco and Tom Potter, Debbie rounded them up in her car, bringing them back to the house when she had a carful, and then going back out again. But in the process of doing all this, she sideswiped a tree, causing significant damage. The car was two weeks old; I have no idea how old the tree was.
5. One of the dogs knocked her over, and she hurt her leg so badly that she could barely walk. (We later found

out she ruptured her Achilles tendon and had to have surgery.)

6. Her bronchitis had worsened.

Then she topped that off with, "But don't worry about anything, you just rest and get better."

No problem, honey.

Bolstered by that cheery news, I didn't get better, but in fact got worse. I moved into full-blown septic shock, and my blood pressure was so low that it barely measured on the machine. A nurse told me that my organs were starting to shut down. The tone of her voice led me to believe that organ-shutting-down is not a good thing.

The doctors, led by Dr. Sean O'Donnell, and the nurses, led by Katrina, Heather, and Sue, were phenomenal. They couldn't have been nicer, and believe me, I was a pain in the ass. They absolutely saved my life and, based on my behavior, they probably had mixed emotions about doing so.

We live in a small town, and everyone knows everything about everyone else. So the staff quickly became aware that I was the semi-famous dog lunatic, and all the nurses began showing me pictures of their dogs and telling me dog anecdotes. One even brought her lab mix in to meet me. That caused me to worry a bit about the sterility of the intensive care environment, because I don't think the dog washed his paws before coming in.

I pretty much complained about everything, with a good amount of whining and moaning thrown in. Tara's stoicism and courage was lost on me; those are traits best left to golden retrievers. By the time I left, after eight days, it's safe to say that none of the hospital personnel were hanging on to my ankles, begging me to stay.

And it seems like everything I said or did while in the hospital became common knowledge in the town. A month after I got out, a woman friend said at dinner, "So I hear you hated the catheter."

Which I did.

I've recovered fully, thanks to Dr. O'Donnell and the staff at Miles Hospital. I doubt that they remember me too fondly. But it's their own fault. If they want courageous patients, they should open a vet hospital and treat golden retrievers.

Senior dogs taught me . . .

what rescue is all about.

Our Tara Foundation did not take in old dogs exclusively, not even close.

It was always a tough call; in fact, which dogs to rescue was always the toughest call of all. We would go into any one of the terrible shelters in the Los Angeles area and there would be between one and two hundred dogs worthy of getting the hell out of there and into someone's loving home.

If we had successfully placed ten that week, then it meant we had ten open spots. The ones we chose would live out their lives happily, and the ones we didn't would likely be put down in the shelter. It was an awful position to be in.

Age was a factor to consider, but it cut a number of ways. The old ones probably had not had a good life up to that point, considering they were dumped in the first place. We wanted to give them some good years; to live the rest of their lives with the love and dignity that they deserved.

But on the other hand, the young ones had probably never experienced any happiness at all, and saving them meant giving them ten or so good years, compared to half that for the seniors. If we were looking to maximize the good years we were providing to dogs in general, then young would be the way to go.

On the third hand was the fact that some young dogs were successfully adopted out of the shelter, but almost never the seniors. People wanted the youthful ones, two years or younger, so leaving them behind was at least not leaving them without any hope.

The fourth hand was that it would take us longer to adopt out the seniors, and since we were limited to twenty-five dog runs at the vet where we kept them, we either would place fewer dogs, or we'd bring more of them home. And even though Debbie has never seemed able to grasp this concept, we had limited space at home as well.

So basically we disregarded all of these factors in choosing dogs, and went with our gut, or more accurately, with Debbie's gut. We didn't set a quota, but my guess is that the seniors wound up comprising about thirty percent of our total. Doing the math, of the four thousand dogs we rescued, maybe twelve hundred were seniors.

And placing them was a challenge. I cannot count how many people would say that they were dog lovers, and to emphasize that fact, would talk about how long and hard they had mourned a pet that had died. They couldn't adopt an older dog, they would claim, because it would die sooner, and they couldn't deal with the grief again. It would be too painful.

Growing up in Paterson, we had an expression that suits this situation.

Tough shit.

If you truly love dogs, and if you are intent on rescue, then don't tell me you can't handle the grief. Because that makes it about you, and rescue is about the dog. Living things die, and if you want to insulate yourself from that fact, then stop visiting your grandmother. Even young dogs have a brief life expectancy compared to humans, so instead of getting a dog, maybe you should get a vase.

There are many reasons to adopt a young dog, or even get a puppy. Maybe you just bond with it, or maybe you live on a beach, or you run a lot in the park, and want a dog who can get the full enjoyment from the surroundings. That is completely fine and understandable and your absolute right. The more good homes for dogs of any age, the better.

I am absolutely not saying that people who adopt seniors are in any way better than those who don't. Just please don't base your decision on the fact that the dog is going to die.

So are you.

We've probably brought four hundred senior dogs into our home, over the years, as our pets. We didn't bring them in because we have a particular love of seniors, though we do. We didn't bring them in because they are smarter, or more obedient, because some are, and some aren't.

We brought them in because they had nowhere else to go. And when they eventually died, it made us feel good to know that for whatever time they were with us, they were happy, and safe, and loved.

So if you want to feel good, one way would be to get a dog for the dog's sake, to save a life that deserves saving. A life that has been difficult but doesn't have to end that way.

Don't let the deciding factor be which one is going to die quicker.

End of lecture.

Rescue dogs taught me . . .

about first impressions.

It was almost twenty years ago that Debbie and I went to dinner at the home of a couple who lived near us in Santa Monica. Debbie had met the woman at her gym, and they had become semi-friends. Neither she nor I had met Alex, her husband.

After dinner, Alex invited me into their game room to play pool. They had an amazing, nine-foot slate pool table; you could get a car for less than it must have cost. Alex handed me a cue and asked me if I wanted to make it interesting by playing for five dollars a game.

Even though I am not aware of a planet on which a five-dollar bet makes a game interesting, and even though I am a terrible pool player, I agreed. He told me not to worry, that he himself hadn't played in years, a claim I doubted. The cues

had relatively fresh chalk on them; somebody had been playing there, and they didn't have any kids.

As bad as I am, Alex was worse. I am a better ballet dancer
and opera singer than he was a pool player. He couldn't put a
ball in a pocket; he was lucky if he kept them on the table. So
I was winning, and he kept bemoaning the fact that he was
rusty from inactivity.

Then he took a shot and once again the ball did not come
close to its intended target. However, it bounced off three sides
and wound up in a pocket at the opposite end of the table. He
nodded solemnly at the result and said, "Some things you
never forget." He was trying to convince me that the ridiculous shot was exactly what he had planned, and represented
some kind of resurrection of his atrophied talent.

With that simple sentence, I knew that Alex was a jerk,
and nothing would ever be able to change my mind. I mentioned this to Debbie on the way home, and she tried to soften
my reaction by saying, "Everyone tries to look good; some
people are just better at it than others." It was a wise, mature
point of view, which is why it had no chance of resonating
with me.

Then along came Harry.

Harry was a beautiful black Newfoundland mix, just a
year and a half old. He was a large, strapping dog that we
found in the West Los Angeles shelter. He ingratiated himself
with Debbie by snuggling up to her when she gave him a bis-
cuit. Then the next day he closed the sale by looking through
the cage at her with pleading eyes that said, "Get me out of
here." Which she did. Immediately.

He was only the fourth dog that we had rescued, having
just started volunteering at the shelter weeks before. We hadn't

even created the Tara Foundation yet, so we had brought the other three dogs home as our pets. We were in an apartment that didn't allow dogs, but that was sort of beside the point.

In any event, Harry wasn't going to be staying with us; we didn't want a dog that young and active, so we were going to bring him home only until we could find a family that would take him in. As a young, beautiful dog, it wouldn't be that hard to do.

As is always the case, the shelter had him neutered before releasing him to us, and I actually drove to their vet's office to get him. Having never seen Harry out of the shelter cage before, I was surprised how mellow he was when I picked him up, but I figured that was a carryover from his surgery.

Dogs in shelter cages sometimes act uncharacteristically wild when they get out, just as a reaction to being cooped up for so long. It makes some more difficult to adopt out than they otherwise would be, because people fear the dog might be too much for them to handle. If the dog is running and jumping crazily at the shelter, they picture him doing that in their living rooms. It's an understandable, albeit uninformed, point of view.

However, for the next three days, Harry remained a study in serenity. He spent the days lying peacefully on a recliner, and often when I sat on a chair or the couch, he would come and rest his head on my knee. When dogs put their head on my knee, the sale is immediately made. I was crazy about him.

On the fourth day, Debbie told me that potential adopters for Harry would be stopping by that night. I responded by saying that I wanted to keep him; that he was the perfect dog. How could we even think of giving our Harry to strangers?

Debbie disagreed, pointing out that we needed to keep

our few household spots available for older dogs, otherwise it would be chaos. I said that Harry was as calm as any older dog. Why should he suffer because he happened to be younger? It was age discrimination, pure and simple.

At the time we had a wonderful eleven-year-old golden retriever named Sophie, who was as sweet and calm as could be. "Harry," I announced solemnly, "is a black Sophie."

Talking Debbie into keeping a dog is not the toughest thing in the world to do. So Harry became a permanent member of our family, and it turned out that his true personality had been suppressed by a post-neutering infection and fever. Once our own vet took care of that, Harry turned into a certifiable maniac.

He invented a lovely little game where he would jump on the couch, then jump off and race across the room, jumping on a recliner chair. Then back to the couch, back to the chair, etc. The game would continue for five or six rounds, or until Harry's 110 pounds knocked the chair back and over. The crash would bring either Debbie or me into the room, and Harry would look at us with some measure of annoyance, barking his demand that we reset the chair so the game could continue.

Harry lived to the age of eleven, and over the years he gradually evolved from a young, insane dog to an old, insane dog. Yet somehow he emerged as one of our favorites, despite not even coming close to living up to his first impression.

Harry was just the beginning. Dogs display one personality when they enter our canine asylum, but it is not a predictor of what they will ultimately become. Only when they are settled and have learned the ropes do we find out what they are really like.

This is especially true of dogs stuck in animal shelters.

They have been through a tremendous ordeal, and need to adjust to a normal life, so that their personality can come out. And the shelter is probably the least of their difficult life experiences, since by definition they can't have been in there long. Their lives must have been very trying before that, or they would not have wound up in the shelter in the first place.

The major factor in their adjustment to normal life has to do with trust, and a golden named Tyson is a perfect example.

We rescued Tyson from the Downey animal shelter in Los Angeles County. If you're a dog that's been abandoned or lost, this particular shelter is not a place where you want to wind up. It's usually overcrowded, and the rate of adoption out of there by the public is very, very low. And when you're eight years old, as Tyson was, the rate moves close to zero.

That is where rescue groups come in, especially for the pure breeds, most of which have their dedicated breed rescues. We rescued all large breeds and mutts, but we were very partial to goldens, and we got Tyson out of there the day he was available.

He was relatively old, and very frail, so we decided to take him straight home to join our crew. To get him into physical shape for someone to want to adopt him would have meant keeping him in a dog run for too long.

But when Tyson got home, he acted as if he longed to be back at Downey. He stayed in a corner of my office, and growled angrily at any dog that wandered by, and of course there is never a moment in our house that dogs aren't wandering by. He even got in three fights when other dogs were not impressed by his growling, though they were easy to break up, and no one got hurt.

He was scared, and he had been in a terrible shelter, and

now he was in a nuthouse, and who knows what had happened to him in his life. Any personality issues he was having were more than understandable. In that kind of situation, we don't put any pressure on the dog; we let him get acclimated in whatever way he likes.

It was an evolving process, but as Tyson got more comfortable, he became more friendly. Within six months he had become a sort of social director for the group; I wouldn't be surprised if, when we weren't around, he was organizing games of charades and Simon Says.

It was a remarkable transformation, and the absolute best thing about rescue. Watching them become less afraid, and feel more safe, is as good as it gets. Then their real personality comes out, and that is never a bad thing.

Well, it's almost never a bad thing. We rescued a six-year-old golden named Bogart from a rescue group, and he fit in immediately. Absolutely no problem; he seemed to like the other dogs, and they liked him.

That didn't last long. He started to get attached to Debbie and I, and then protective of us. His behavior started as growling, and then flared up into fights. In the third fight, I reached in to grab Bogart's collar to pull him away (the wrong approach), and he turned and bit me, probably thinking I was another dog, and a threat to him.

It left me with twenty-one stitches, and we had to return Bogart to the rescue group. It was one of the few times that an adoption didn't work out, but there was nothing we could do. The advantage of getting a dog from a rescue group, compared to a shelter, is that if the dog doesn't work out for whatever reason, you can return it to the rescue group without fear of anything bad happening to it. In fact, rescue groups insist that you sign a contract agreeing to return the dog if you don't want to keep it, for whatever reason.

So I've learned that first impressions can be dramatically wrong, and I try to avoid them.

But I still think Alex the pool player is a jerk.

Irish and Bernie taught me . . .

there's weather and then there's *weather*.

I will confess that I never liked living in Southern California. I thought I'd get used to it, but after twenty years it seemed clear that it was not going to happen.

The weather was one of the things I couldn't get used to, basically because there wasn't any. For nine months a year, every day was basically the same, sunny with no chance of anything other than sunny. Precipitation probability: completely nonexistent.

At the end of the weather forecasts on the local news, they would show the upcoming seven days, each with a symbol of a sun, as well as the projected high and low temperature. I remember one time when the highs on successive days were going to be 84, 82, 85, 83 . . . and the weather person said that the upcoming week was going to be a "roller coaster."

The only notable thing about the weather forecasts in California was the forecasters themselves. They were almost exclusively beautiful women, mostly blondes, all with great figures. I spent many a day regretting the fact that I hadn't gone to meteorology school.

But I digress.

On those rare occasions when there was rain, usually between January and March, the local news stations moved into emergency mode. They would run banners proclaiming it STORM WATCH 2011, and would divide the screen into quadrants. Each quadrant had some poor reporter standing outside with an umbrella, reporting that it was in fact raining in Glendale, Torrance, Hollywood, and Venice. Close-ups would provide unnecessary confirmation by showing the raindrops hitting the existing puddles. They covered the rain the way cable news covers Kim Kardashian.

Compelling stuff.

I wanted to enjoy the few occasions when it rained hard, but felt too guilty to do so. Because there were always wildfires, which destroyed vegetation, there was nothing left to absorb the water, so when there was precipitation, mudslides were the result. It's pretty hard to take pleasure in the rain when the newscasts were showing houses being washed away in a sea of mud.

One of the fondest memories of my childhood growing up in Paterson, New Jersey, was sitting on our front porch during thunderstorms, watching the rain bounce off the street. In addition to revealing that I was a pretty boring kid back then, it helps explain why I disliked the lack of California weather so much.

It also reveals one of the major reasons we moved to

Maine, a state that has always been chock-full of weather. Actually having four seasons was irresistible to me, and even to Debbie, who was born in Pennsylvania and lived in New York for many years. All of our Californian friends thought we were nuts, which probably explains why they are still there.

We got to Maine in September, and it was during a surprise early snowstorm in late October that we realized we had hit canine climate gold. The snow had no sooner started to fall than our gang began going through the doggie door like it was New York City's outbound Lincoln Tunnel during rush hour.

We have about three acres of woods fenced off, and the dogs covered every inch of them. It was the first time they had shown a real desire to spend any time out there, and it was remarkable. They simply would not come inside as long as it was snowing, and the colder it was, the better.

Bernie the Bernese mountain dog was particularly hilarious. He lay down on the ground, a look of pure joy on his face, and just let the snow fall on him. When he got covered almost to the point where we couldn't see him, he got up and shook himself off. Then he lay back down and started the process all over again. He's repeated the same routine many times since.

This behavior of all the dogs continued from that point on, and snow wasn't even necessary. Almost every one of them just loves the freezing weather; the difference in the amount of time they spend outdoors in winter compared to summer is amazing.

Debbie was of course delighted that they were so happy, and so was I, though I characteristically was able to extract something negative from it. I felt guilty that we had kept them in Southern California so long, and thought about how many dogs we had that never lived long enough to experience the glorious cold.

The bottom line is you can trust me when I tell you this: a dog is only better off in California than Maine if he surfs, skateboards, or if he's in the movie business.

Our first summer in Maine came around, and while I was on a book tour, Debbie got a phone call from a shelter in Waterville, saying that they had a nine-year-old golden retriever named Irish who needed a home. I have no idea how they heard of us or got our number, since Waterville is fairly far from us.

But they reached Debbie, and she was probably in the car before she even hung up the phone, and within a few hours Irish was a member of our family.

We quickly discovered that there was no way Irish was nine years old; he was at least three years younger. Shelters often tell us a dog is older than he or she is, knowing that we're more likely to take in an old dog, thinking that it would be harder for the shelter to find him a home. It's the opposite of the norm; usually shelters will shade the age in the opposite direction, claiming the dog is younger than its actual age, since that would make most people more inclined to adopt.

But in all other respects Irish was a typical golden, friendly, smart, and loving. He barked a lot, which didn't exactly make him unique in our group. But he was and is a terrific addition to the clan.

And then came our first thunderstorm. I was excited by the forecast, and I loved it when the skies turned completely dark, and 4:00 P.M. looked like 8:00 P.M. The only negative was that the satellite television went out.

Well, maybe that wasn't the only negative. Irish was not as

pleased as I by the change in weather. He started to run around the house like he was the ball in a pinball machine, wild-eyed and panting heavily. Debbie realized that he was sensing the thunder and lightning even before it came, just as Tara had sensed the Northridge earthquake before we felt a thing, many years before.

I took Irish in my office and closed the door, hoping I'd be able to hold and calm him. It didn't quite work out that way, at least not once the thunder started in earnest.

He took a running leap and crashed through the screen in my open office window, and ran down our driveway. I ran after him, but there was no catching him; he was out of sight in moments.

I ran back toward the house and went inside. First I wanted to close the window, so no other dogs could escape through the smashed screen. It turned out not to be an issue; they had no more desire to run out into the monsoon than I did. We have not raised stupid dogs.

Then I wanted to get the car keys so I could search for Irish. With how spread out our neighborhood is, consisting of very few houses set in the middle of thick woods, I wasn't terribly hopeful of finding him. Not the way he was running. Having one of our dogs lost and unprotected, especially with all the wild animals out there in the woods, is a sickening feeling.

But I didn't have to find him; one of our neighbors did. The phone rang just as I was leaving, and it was Tom Potter, a terrific and helpful guy who lives about a quarter mile away. While Irish had gone through our screen to the outside, he had thought better of it and reversed course at Tom's house. He had run straight through their screen door, into the house.

I wasn't quite sure why Irish wanted out of our house and

into Tom's, but I didn't have time to be offended. I drove over there, and Tom couldn't have been nicer. He had held on to Irish to prevent him from running off again, and together we got the panting dog into my car. I took his screen door with me; the least I could do was get it repaired.

The weird thing is that all of our California dogs, who very rarely if ever had heard thunder in their lives, were fine in the storm. Irish, a Mainer all the way, had been the only one to go nuts. And it continues to this day; we've tried a bunch of remedies, but every time we have a thunderstorm he freaks out. We have, however, learned to keep the windows closed.

So summer is by far the least pleasant time here for both the dogs and myself. We've got heat, and humidity, and ticks, and mosquitos, and tourists, and Irish freaking out from the thunder.

And then there is the house-training, which decreases proportionately with the amount of rain. In the winter we can go months without an accident in the house. In the summer, when it's raining, we're lucky if we go minutes.

And, of course, Debbie sees the problem differently than I do. When we first discover that somebody has pissed in the house, she asks me, "Who did it?" It's as if she's skeptical that one of the dogs could be guilty of such a thing, and perhaps I did it to get them in trouble.

"I don't know. I'll run a DNA test," I usually snarl.

That prompts her to say, "With this much rain, I don't blame them for not wanting to go outside."

I do.

Sky and Otis taught me . . .

the importance of teamwork.

The dogs generally wake us up with their barking between five thirty and six o'clock in the morning. The time fluctuates by season; when it's light earlier they are more inclined to get up. And once they're up, the idea of humans sleeping really annoys them.

But whatever time they actually force us out of bed, I believe that they must schedule a meeting among themselves a half hour earlier. That way they can go over the daily schedule, and assign their members to specific jobs.

Because they are nothing if not organized.

I'm not sure who the leader is, though my best guess is Jenny, a lab mix who is definitely a Type A personality. But whether it is Jenny or one of the other ones, there must be a structure by which assignments are given. They're like a Fortune 500 company, without the fortune.

There is always one dog whose job it is to do something irritating. For example, Jenny herself is the first to bark every morning, possibly because she is able to do so from a unique vantage point. She sleeps with her head on my pillow, and is thus able to bark directly into my ear. That would be more than sufficient to wake me, though her one bark is all it takes to set off her colleagues in a supportive barking frenzy.

They know the drill; when Jenny gives the signal, barking commences, and it doesn't stop until I am downstairs and putting out the food. I actually fill the dishes with food the night before, so as to be able to get into the feeding faster, thereby stopping the barking.

A similar situation exists regarding visitors to the house. By this I don't mean people actually coming inside; there are a limited number of people crazy enough to attempt that. I'm talking more about people like FedEx or UPS employees, who pull into our driveway to make a delivery.

We used to have a white shepherd named Sky who was turned in to a California rescue group because he would go wild whenever anyone approached the house that he and his family were living in. One time he got out and in his frenzy nipped a child, though she was not hurt. The neighbors got upset, and tried to have Sky put down. Fortunately, the rescue group saved him and gave him to us. It was one of our best rescues ever.

But while Sky was a wonderful dog, he truly lost it when he saw someone outside. If the gardener would come and work for three hours, then Sky would bark for three hours. All the time he would track the gardener's whereabouts, barking at the window closest to where he was. It's fair to say that we didn't look forward to gardener days.

Sky's barking would initially set the others off, though their participation in the noisemaking was intermittent. Sky was annoying enough on his own, so his canine colleagues seemed willing to let him do the heavy lifting. As long as Sky was successfully torturing us with his barking, there was no real reason for them to join in.

But Sky had a physical problem; on two different occasions he tore an ACL, one on each of his back legs. This necessitated fairly major surgeries, each of which he came through just fine. But his recovery, like everything else in our house, was complicated.

The surgeon was quite clear; Sky was to have no physical activity of any kind for six weeks after the operations. There was simply no way to ensure this in our environment; he just had too many friends to play with. So after each surgery Sky had to stay at the vet's office for the full six weeks, in a confined area, so they could monitor him and see to it that he healed correctly and well.

If Sky was Wally Pipp, then a shepherd mix named Otis was Lou Gehrig. During the time Sky was at the vet's office, Otis, who previously had shown little interest in the gardener or any other visitor, heroically stepped in and filled the breach. He became Sky's worthy successor, barking maniacally at anyone and everyone who appeared outside the house. Otis was always a little bit nuts, but he really stepped up and expanded his game when Sky went down.

Sky died at eleven years old of what appeared to be a heart attack; we found him lying on the guest room bed one morning. It's very jarring to have a dog die unexpectedly in the house, an experience we've probably had a dozen times. But all things considered, it's a great way to go. I don't think Sky suffered at all; the night before his death he ate a big meal and seemed fine.

Otis was four at the time, and he has continued to fill Sky's role of resident lunatic ever since. He's nine now, an age when he's probably grooming his successor. I don't know who that might be, but there is no shortage of candidates.

The house we have in Maine is the first one that we've lived in that has more than one level. We've tried to keep stairs to a minimum, because our old dogs have trouble navigating them. But this house was so perfect for them, and us, that we made an exception. There are only two rooms on the second floor, our bedroom and an exercise room.

When we first got here, a golden mix named Simon would position himself at the landing at the top of the steps. He'd growl at other dogs as they'd attempt to get by and into the bedroom. They'd either be afraid of him, or they'd just bark in a vain attempt to get him to relent and let them pass. A few of the braver and larger ones simply called his bluff and walked right past him, and he was smart enough not to intervene.

But the situation became untenable, especially since there was a constant risk of a fight, so we trained Simon not to stay there, luring him away with biscuits, and setting up a comfortable spot for him in the bedroom.

But of course this left the staircase position unmanned, so one of our Pyrenees, Boomer, gallantly stepped up and filled the role. And it's a lot tougher to get around Boomer, who is twice Simon's size. At night, the top-of-the-stairs bouncer job goes to Ralph, who apparently needs less sleep than Boomer.

Besides, Boomer prefers sleeping in bed with us, so he's willing to give up the spot on the stairs.

I think they must assign the jobs on a seniority basis; the ones who have been here the longest get their pick of the assignments. There must be a foreman who makes the decisions.

So whatever the task, whether it's having accidents in the house, occupying my favorite recliner and refusing to give it back, or drooling in the water dishes, one dog fulfills the responsibility for the whole gang.

Our dogs form a well-oiled machine, displaying the kind of teamwork that CEOs and football coaches only dream of instilling in their teams.

These dogs don't do it for the glory. Or the biscuits. Or the petting.

No, they do it to annoy me.

All the dogs taught me . . .

all about shit bags.

My working career prior to becoming a writer was in the movie business. I was president of marketing, which is not exactly a power position within the industry. Rather, that power usually resided either with executives above me, or big-time producers, directors, or stars.

Many of these people were not always tactful, or pleasant, or particularly supportive, especially when their films opened badly. And in my less-than-capable hands, quite a few films opened badly. Since these were not the type of people inclined to blame themselves, the marketing person, in this case me, became the obvious scapegoat.

I'm certainly not looking for sympathy; I was well paid, and I'm sure people in many other industries and careers are in the same position. You've got a lot of people to answer to, and your job is to make them happy. If you don't, one thing is for sure: *You take a lot of shit.*

Animal rescue is different, and probably unique. When you rescue animals and have them in your home, you don't take a lot of shit, you pick it up. And trust me, that isn't much more fun.

Picking up dog shit is no different than any other artistic profession; technique is crucial to the process. And there is no shortage of techniques; it's really a matter of personal preference. But the bottom line is this: you are judged at the end by how much is in the bag, and how much is on the ground.

Debbie is a maestro at it. She is a bender and a swiper, moving the bag effortlessly down and across, so in an eye blink the "material" is magically removed, before she goes on to the next one. And in our yard, there is always a next one. And a one after that.

She is fast and very thorough, much more so than me. She can't stand to leave anything behind, even though she is keenly aware that more will be deposited very quickly. When she's finished with the removal, and then the hosing down, she happily pronounces the yard to be "pristine." It is always a poignant moment.

I, on the other hand, am a shoveler . . . literally. I use a snow shovel, pushing everything to the fence, so it can then be scooped up and deposited into bags. I do it this way because I've had four back surgeries and can't bend very well, and because I'm lazy. The yard doesn't wind up perfect, which I have no problem with.

But whatever our respective techniques and strategies,

one thing Debbie and I agree on is the absolute need to have state-of-the-art tools at our disposal, especially when it comes to plastic bags. As disgusting as it is to maneuver the shit into the bags, it would be even more revolting to have the bag unable to support the accumulated weight, and have the bottom open up.

Trust me . . . been there, done that.

Most supermarket bags are simply not up to the task. It pains me to say it, but as a country we are woefully lacking in shit bag design and material, well behind our counterparts in Western Europe, and probably wherever they have elephants. I'm not sure why that is, other than our best and brightest students seem to choose science, technology, and math over a career in shit bags.

It's not a big deal if you have a Pomeranian, or a Maltese; in those cases a tissue is really all you need. But when you have upward of twenty large dogs, as we do, Kleenex just won't cut it.

There is an upscale chain of supermarkets in Southern California called Gelson's, and their bags are excellent . . . firm and strong. When we would shop there, we'd get as many bags as we could, surreptitiously grabbing a bunch as we left. But we never got enough.

Then we had the idea that maybe we could go in and just buy the bags, and sure enough, they sold cases of them to us. They'd always ask why, and we'd tell them the truth, embarrassing as it was. But it worked fine, and the bags were up to the task. Life was good, and the yard was clean.

Then, when we moved to Orange County, we found shit bag Nirvana. The bags at Pacific Ranch Market in Orange,

California, put Gelson's to shame. Watching Debbie use them in the yard brought tears to my eyes; she finally had the tools to match her considerable talents.

So when we moved to Maine, we were understandably worried. Maine is not exactly a hotbed of science and research; suppose they were behind in the crucial area of shit bag development? If you've ever seen our mastiff Wanda take a dump, you'd know what a nightmare that would be.

So before we left, we bought three cases of bags from Pacific Ranch, and moved them to Maine. They wouldn't last forever, but that was all the manager would sell us.

Fast forward three years, and we had almost run out, down to about a six-month supply. Worse yet, the grocery stores in Maine were as shit bag backward as we had feared. I've tried to analyze the reason for that. I think it's because while the answer to the question "Do bears shit in the woods?" is "Yes," no one has to pick it up.

In any event, we were facing a crisis, and something had to be done. We had two choices; either replenish the bag supply, or stop feeding the dogs.

Mercifully, I was to be in California on a book tour for *Hounded,* an Andy Carpenter mystery. I carved out enough time to drive down to Pacific Ranch and went in to buy some cases. The manager I spoke with was not one that I remembered, and he was initially reluctant to make the sale, since they use their bags for other purposes, such as carrying groceries. As he pondered his decision I could feel my heart pounding, and I'm not ashamed to say that I was prepared to beg, but it turned out not to be necessary. He finally agreed to sell me two cases, and each case had fifteen hundred bags.

I took them to a UPS store to ship them back to Maine. I guess there are certain questions the clerks have to ask, so she questioned what was in the boxes. I indelicately blurted out "shit bags" and since I'm not sure that UPS willingly ships shit, I had to explain what I meant.

Smiling and continuing with her obligatory questions, she asked me if I wanted to insure them. I declined, telling her that their value was substantial but sentimental. And then I left, sending them on their mission. When those bags were born, they probably thought they'd be carrying tomatoes, or apples.

Little did they know.

So now we have two cases, which might last two years or so. You'll know when we run out, because I'll be announcing a California book tour right around that time.

Update: Literally days after I wrote this chapter, California announced a ban on all plastic bags. Our worst nightmare has come to pass.

All the dogs taught me . . .

that the world has gotten smaller,
and we are all connected.

For a good portion of the time we were running the Tara Foundation in Southern California, the Internet was a fledgling operation. We didn't even have a Web site, and we advertised for potential adopters in the old-fashioned way, by taking out classified ads in the *Los Angeles Times.*

Now, of course, it's far easier and much cheaper to reach the people you want to online, but back then we didn't have that option.

My first experience with the power of the Internet as it comes to dogs and dog rescue was when our house was in the area where a raging wildfire was happening, and we were evacuated. We wound up spending eight days in a hotel, during which we were sure the house could not have survived the flames that were approaching as we fled.

While in the hotel, I received an e-mail from a dog rescuer back east, not someone I had ever met, and I told her that we probably lost our house, and that we'd have to move our twenty-seven dogs to our newly purchased home in Maine.

Since she had identified herself as a dog person, I asked her if she had any idea how we could accomplish that move.

She must have put the question out into cyberspace, because in the next three days I received 171 e-mails from strangers, telling us that we could use their house if they were on the route on our way to Maine, that they would put us (and of course all the dogs) up in their homes. It was remarkable, but it was my first inkling of the way the Internet had managed to connect dog lunatics everywhere.

Our house survived, thanks to heroic work by the firefighters. It's lucky it did, because our move to Maine would have been a disaster. When we bought the house in Maine, we were told it was a year-round, winterized building, even though many houses on our lake are not.

Five years later, when we were finally ready to move and consulted with a contractor about renovations, he told us that among other things the windows and heating system would have to be upgraded to survive the winters. When we told him the previous owner lived there year-round, he said that if he did, then "his body is frozen in the basement."

Of course, since I'm an "Internet-half-empty" person, I choose to focus on the negative aspects of its effect on our rescue work. For example, now that I am fairly well known as a dog nut, everybody sends me funny or touching dog videos that circulate online.

I actually sort of like those videos, but there is a seemingly unending supply of them; there must be half a million. And of course, since they've all gone viral or near viral, I probably receive each one from fifty different people. Half a million videos . . . fifty times . . . you do the math.

But I can hit the delete button with the best of them, so it's a manageable problem. More serious and troubling are the people who ask me to take in dogs.

Because of *Dogtripping*, ours is known as a home that welcomes old or infirm large dogs; they are pretty much the only types we will take. And those are obviously the toughest to find homes for, which is why we started taking them in the first place.

But the Internet now empowers people from all over the country to tell us about dogs that they think would be perfect for our house, and in fact many are. We have taken in dogs from Texas, and Kentucky, and Upstate New York, and New Jersey, and Arizona . . . you get the picture, and we get the dogs.

Of course, we're getting older, and I'm getting lazier, so pretty much every twenty minutes we make a vow to not take any more dogs in, with the goal of reducing our number through attrition. The problem is that it's so damn hard to say no.

Just about all of our friends here in Maine are dog lovers, and one of them, Diane Ranes, was looking for a third dog for her house. She went online to search for likely candidates, and found one on the Web site of a rescue group in Upstate New York. There was a photo and description of the dog, a Maremma named Molly, and she sent the Web site link to Debbie, to get her opinion.

Sending a rescue Web site link to Debbie is almost as bad as driving her to a dog shelter. She simply has no self-control in such situations. She looked at Molly's information, which described her as unsocialized and basically feral; she had literally been found running wild in a forest. For various reasons Debbie didn't think Molly would make a good candidate for Diane's house, and told her so.

Of course, that wasn't the end of it. Debbie started browsing around on the site, and came upon seven-year-old Great Pyrenees sisters. They were beautiful, and looked sweet, and the next day I found myself driving eight hours (sixteen hours round-trip) to Utica, New York, to pick them up. Their names were Boomer and Cheyenne.

And they were terrific in our home with the other dogs. When we got them they were very matted, so much so that it would have been painful for them to be brushed out. It was summertime, so we shaved them. The groomer left their full hair on the head and face, so with the rest of their body shaved, they looked like twin Q-tips.

After a week the rescue group called, as they are wont to do, to find out how things were with Boomer and Cheyenne. Debbie described how perfectly they fit in, and how we already loved them.

But almost as bad as taking Debbie to a shelter, or giving her a rescue group link, is having her talk to the head of such a group. Lo and behold, the conversation got around to "feral" Molly, and lo-er and behold-er, the next day I found myself driving back to Utica to pick her up as well.

When I got there, Molly took one look at me and tried to run, resisting my attempts to get her in the car. It was a re-creation of my experiences with pretty much every girl I knew in high school.

When I got her home it was more of the same. She hid

behind the desk in my office and came out only to go to the "bathroom" outside and eat. It seemed like it was going to be a long haul.

Fast forward a year to now, and she often sleeps on our bed, is a full-fledged member of the pack, and seems to be loving life.

As for Diane Ranes, even though she is a highly intelligent woman with a Ph.D., she claims to have had no idea that sending Debbie the link would result in our getting two hundred fifty pounds of dogs.

I secretly think she colluded with Debbie all along, but I don't hold it against her for doing it. Debbie, of course, praises her to the skies for bringing such great dogs into our house. And they really are terrific—all three of them.

We're still trying to cut back on our number, so please, if you're reading this, do not ask me to take in another dog. Much more important, do not ask Debbie.

I really don't want to have to drive back to Utica.

Tara taught me . . .

to appreciate the little things in life.

W ell, she tried to anyway, but it didn't take. Life appreciation doesn't seem to be my style.

There were two basic walks we took Tara on. One was through the Hollywood Hills, which is where Debbie and I were living at the time. The other was in Beverly Hills; we would drive there and make a large loop, starting at Beverly Drive.

The Hollywood Hills walk, as you might imagine, included a lot of hills. But the Beverly Hills walk, in the area that we were, was flat. When it comes to walking, I have a strong preference for flat. Actually I prefer downhill, but it's rather hard to find a round-trip walk that is exclusively downhill.

The point of the walks was Tara, and that was basically the reason I left my favorite recliner chair to go on them. Tara just loved to walk with us, and the excitement she showed any time we went near the leash was impossible to resist.

In the nine months or so that I knew Tara before she became ill, I'd say we went on each of those walks maybe fifty times. It was usually both Debbie and I that were with her, but on those occasions when Debbie was out of town on business, it was just me.

So there was a sameness to the surroundings; we were not breaking new ground. Yet to watch Tara, you would never know that each time was not her first time. She missed nothing and explored everything. She smelled every blade of grass, and then she rolled in them. If there was a puddle of water, she jumped in it like it was the Pacific Ocean. Her ears perked up at every sound, regardless of how commonplace it was, and she was maybe the cutest ear-perker in America.

When we came upon another dog, and we ran into the same dogs and owners frequently, it was as if she were making a new, exciting friend each time. They would sniff each other pretty much all over.

It was a way of behaving that was completely foreign to me. My idea of keeping in close contact with friends is to send e-mails and leave messages on one another's voice mails. When I meet new people, I'm much more reserved; I can't remember the last time I met someone new and immediately sniffed their ass.

The point is that Tara could find joy in anything and everything. During the day she had it down to a science; she spent all her time either enjoying herself, or sleeping. I combine the two . . . I enjoy sleeping. The rest of the time I'm a cranky pain in the butt.

But finding enjoyment was certainly not unique to Tara; it's a dog thing. I would say that it takes so little to make them happy, but that's not the best way to describe it. They come "pre-happy"; it's their default mood. Humans can accentuate their own happiness, or diminish it, or even ruin it, but in dogs it's baked in.

In California we had a golden retriever named Gypsy. In fact, at the time we had two golden retrievers named Gypsy, since they already had the names when we got them as adults. One was light colored, quite old, and relatively inactive because of that age.

The other Gypsy was a dark red color, almost like an Irish setter. She was six years old and thought she was two, with as much energy as I've ever seen in a dog that age. She was wild and crazy, just playful. Very, very, very playful.

Our property sloped down a hill, and at the bottom there was a riding ring for horses, though we didn't have any. So it was just an open area that the dogs could run around in, if they were so inclined. Most of the time the dogs ambled down there in the morning, then worked their way back to have breakfast. We called it their morning constitutional.

One day I was at the top of the hill and saw Gypsy down in the riding area. I took a tennis ball and threw it down there, a distance of maybe a hundred and fifty feet. She ran to where she judged it would land, leaped, and caught it in her mouth. It was an amazing catch.

Then she ran it all the way up the hill, dropped it at my feet, and ran back down. She did everything but say, "Hey, moron, you just keep throwing the ball, and I'll keep catching it."

She would do this endlessly, or at least it would have been endlessly if I didn't get tired of throwing it. I can't imagine how many miles she ran, up and down the hill, while playing this game. Not only was she tireless, but she was amazingly proficient. We continued to call her Gypsy, because that's the name she knew, but when Debbie and I talked about her, we referred to her as Willie Mays.

One day Gypsy seemed out of sorts and uncharacteristically inactive. Seemingly overnight she had developed a bad hot spot, which goldens are prone to. It's an inflammation of the skin, and they often chew their hair away from the spot, attempting to lick at it.

It was very ugly, and I assumed that it was infected, which was causing her to not feel well. I took her to our vet, and was stunned to learn that it was a cancerous tumor that had broken through the skin. It was the first time I had ever seen anything like it, and fortunately I haven't again since.

The vet knew with certainty that she would never again have an acceptable quality of life, and we made the only possible decision under the circumstances, which was to put her down. It is always a hard thing to do, always, but in this case it was even harder.

We were ending the life of a dog that was relatively young, and who enjoyed that life so thoroughly. On a personal note, it was made even harder by the fact that I wasn't expecting to have to do it. Usually I can tell when a dog is at or near the end, and prepare myself. But this time I had no idea, so it was not only sad, but a shock as well.

If I was to look on the positive side, which is to say if I was like Debbie, I would say that Gypsy loved life right until the end, and never had to suffer with her cancer the way most goldens do. I'd say that she felt fine yesterday, running and playing, and today she died.

But that wouldn't be me. Instead I mentally berated myself for not discovering Gypsy's love of playing catch earlier. We only had her for a year, which meant I wasted nine months not playing the game with her.

They try their best to tell us, to mold us. When you happen to do something that particularly pleases them, maybe scratch them in the perfect spot, they wag their tail, and get a smile on their face. So sometimes we catch on, and are able to give them what they want.

It's one of the few frustrations I find in rescuing senior dogs. They've spent their whole lives revealing their preferences, and hopefully getting them noticed and provided. But I haven't been there for that, so I have to figure it out. And by definition with seniors, there isn't that much time to do so, especially since we have so many dogs to occupy our attention.

Gypsy is the perfect example. It took time for her to tell me what she wanted, but I wish I had known so much earlier.

More than anything else, I wish I knew how to know.

Mamie taught me . . .

it doesn't pay to be nice.

M amie hates me. I've had goldens that were afraid of me, that barked at me, that wouldn't let me pet them. But I've never before had one that hated me. Mamie hates me.

I feed her. I clean up after her. I take her to the groomer. I give her life-sustaining medicine. I take her to the vet. But she hates me.

Mamie is probably fourteen years old. I was in Houston about five years ago for a book signing, and while I was there Debbie was notified that there was a nine-year-old golden in the awful East Valley shelter that was about to be put down.

Going to shelters was always my job, but since I was not around, Debbie e-mailed and told me she was going. I braced for the worst, since Debbie goes to shelters like some people go to Neiman Marcus; she's an animal shelter shopaholic.

Sure enough, she brought home four dogs that day, a Border collie mix, a black lab mix, Wanda the mastiff, and Mamie. So in that sense, Mamie is responsible for us getting three other great dogs. That's the only positive thing I will say about her.

She spends the entire day in my office, lying about four feet from my desk. I think she does this because she once overheard Michael Corleone say, "Keep your friends close, but your enemies closer."

Mamie has bitten me four times. Not really bad head-for-the-hospital bites; she's actually only broken the skin once. It usually happens when I walk by her and startle her, so Debbie takes her side in the argument. But the point I can't seem to get across to her is that I walk by and startle a lot of dogs, yet Mamie is the only one that chooses to bite me. Besides, my going to my desk and sitting down shouldn't be all that startling; I spend a lot of time there.

Even more egregious, from my point of view, is her tendency to piss in the kitchen. The kitchen is between my office and the doggie door, and on the way outside, Mamie will occasionally stop to squat and relieve herself on the kitchen floor.

But it only happens when I'm home, and usually only when I'm watching. She sees me looking at her, gives me a half smile, and squats. It's as if she is saying, "I'm pissing in the kitchen, and I don't care if you like it or not, because I don't like you. So get some towels and clean it up, sucker."

Mamie is my avowed enemy. When I was in critical condition in the hospital, one of the scariest things about it was the knowledge that Mamie might outlive me. I hated giving her the satisfaction.

Of course, it's not like in her dealings that do not include me she's all sunshine and roses. This is a really old dog, who has trouble getting up, and little mobility when she does. Except for Bumper, every dog in our house could kick her golden ass.

But they're scared to death of her. If Wanda is in my office, and Mamie is lying between her and the kitchen, Wanda will walk all the way around the house so as not to have to go by Mamie. And Wanda is not alone in that; all of them are afraid of Mamie's wrath, should they make the mistake of wandering by her.

The most remarkable thing is something that happened recently during medicine time. Seven dogs are on liquid pain meds, which I put on bread. All the dogs like bread, so I give everyone pieces of it, not just the medicine recipients.

If by accident I drop a piece of bread on the floor, a scrum ensues, as all of them dive for it. It's the time when a fight would be most likely to break out, though that hasn't happened yet. But the other day, when I went to give Mamie her bread, I accidentally dropped it on the floor.

Nothing happened.

Nobody moved.

Everybody was afraid to go after Mamie's bread, so she calmly bent down and took it off the floor, chewing it slowly, daring anyone to mess with her.

She is evil and she has to be stopped.

Of course, Debbie's experiences with her are slightly different. For instance, when Debbie sits in the den watching television or reading, Mamie walks up to her and nestles her head against Debbie's leg, so that Debbie can scratch her ears. If I were to try to scratch Mamie's ears, I would be typing these words with stumps instead of fingers.

And then, one day, it all changed. Mamie was sick, throwing up and obviously feeling terrible. I put her in the car to take her to the vet. I knew from experience that she would only sit in the front passenger seat; if I put her in the back she would climb into the front.

And that was fine with me, because I like to have her in the front, where I can see her. I'm sure you've noticed that I use a lot of *Godfather* references, but another one seems necessary here. Both Paulie and Carlo were killed by someone behind them, in the backseat. I'm not about to give Mamie that advantage.

So there she was, sitting next to me and clearly ill. The time when I most intensely bond with dogs is when they are not feeling well, and they have to depend on me to get them care and protect them.

At that moment, Mamie looked so sad that I took a chance and petted her, and she let me! Then she moved toward me and laid her head on my arm. So I petted her again, and she let me again! It was practically a love fest.

It turned out that Mamie was pretty sick; she had pancreatitis, and had to stay at the vet's office on fluids and antibiotics for a few days. When I went to pick her up, she was the old Mamie, feeling good, irascible, and obnoxious.

From that day until this one, we are back to being natural enemies. She still lies near me in my office, glaring at me, daring me to walk by.

I don't remind her about that moment of warmth we shared. I don't have to. She remembers.

And I'll bet it's killing her.

Heh, heh, heh.

Every day Bumper teaches me . . .

all about guts.

I wrote about Bumper in *Dogtripping,* and the fact that I'm doing so again is really all you need to know about him.

He's a dog we got from a rescue group in Louisville, a beautiful three-year-old blond golden who suffered from grand mal seizures. The people who had him in foster care there, Pat and Dick Fish, actually drove him from Louisville to Albuquerque, where I was doing a book signing, and I then drove him home to California.

For the next four years he continued to suffer occasional bouts of those seizures, and they were the most violent and horrifying I have ever seen. We had him on heavy medication, phenobarbital and potassium bromide, but they just couldn't fully control his disease. It was torture to watch him go through the seizures. We've probably had a dozen epileptic dogs over the years, and have three now, but none of them had it anything like Bumper.

About six years ago, when Debbie and I were away, he had an attack so bad that he had to be hospitalized, and nearly died. For two weeks after he finally came home, he was like a zombie, unresponsive and seemingly unaware of his surroundings. We'd find him lying out on the property, which was totally uncharacteristic, and I'd have to carry him back to the house. We thought for sure that we were going to lose him, and on more than one occasion considered putting him out of what seemed to be his misery.

Then he just snapped out of it, and the way I realized it was that he was waiting for us on the bed one night when we were ready to go to sleep. The fact that he had been able to make the jump onto the bed was something we never thought we'd see again.

And that was it. He never had another seizure again, not one. It was like he had his youth back, and the next few years were great ones for him. At our vet's suggestion, I've kept him on the meds, since they don't affect his behavior or personality, and since I'm afraid if I stop he'll have a relapse.

Bumper is fourteen now, and he has slowed down considerably. When I say "slowed down," I mean it literally, and I am drastically understating the case. There is plant life that moves faster than he does.

Like many senior goldens, Bumper has severe arthritis, and he's on heavy pain meds. I have no idea how he is able to get up, but he does it, without fail. It takes him probably three or four minutes to walk fifteen feet, but he does that, too, unaided.

And he keeps eating, and smiling.

We watch Bumper like a hawk, wondering if each day will, or should, be his last. We are committed to not letting him suffer, but he keeps defying the odds.

Our basic rule, which we've developed over time, is if the dog is eating and able to get up on his own, he has a quality of life and we would not consider putting him down. Dogs generally will not eat when they are in pain, or feeling awful.

So even though it bothers us to watch Bumper shuffle along, it would feel like a betrayal to end his life. He likes hanging with the other dogs, and he is willing to put in the effort to do so. If he is going to display this kind of guts and courage, we are not going to deprive him of the opportunity.

By the time this book comes out, I seriously doubt that we will still have the great Bumper. But I've been wrong before, and I hope he proves me wrong again.

*The California contingent tried to
teach me to . . .*

make the best of it.

A nd failed. I wrote *Dogtripping* about our caravan from
California to our new home in Maine. It was a rather
complicated endeavor, mainly because we had twenty-five
dogs that were making the trip with us.

We literally spent five years trying to figure out the best way
to do it, ultimately settling on three RVs. Of course it would
have been fairly difficult for Debbie and I to drive three RVs
by ourselves, and fortunately we found ourselves with nine
human volunteers, from all over the country. There were only
a few friends in this group; many of the people were readers
of my books that we hadn't even met.

There was a very substantial amount of planning involved,
concerning the route, where and whether we would sleep, eat,

etc. We also had to figure out how we would walk the dogs, because to fail to do so might have left the RVs a tad gamey by the time we got as far as Nevada.

Contingencies had to be thought of and planned for. What if a dog got loose and ran off? Or needed veterinary care? What if an RV broke down? We never really came up with acceptable answers for what we would do in some of these hypotheticals, but we did our best.

I would have never been able to plan this stuff on my own; I wouldn't even have attempted it. If left solely up to me, we'd be in some ditch in Iowa right now. But a woman named Cyndi Flores filled the breach. She became the captain of the team, and I happily deferred to her on all major issues.

The attitude and condition of the dogs were a major concern. Without exception these were senior dogs who had no doubt lived rough lives before we got them. Finally they came to us and settled in, comfortably and safely, in a loving home. The act of putting them in RVs for five days, dramatically changing their lifestyle and environment, was bound to be emotionally stressful.

The physical aspect was going to be difficult for them as well. You can search long and hard and not find a large, senior dog without arthritis. Going up and down the narrow, steep steps of the RV was going to be very difficult, and so was sleeping and resting in smaller and more confined spaces than they were used to.

We brought two hundred feet of rolled-up plastic fencing, which we would unfurl each time the dogs had to be walked, in the process setting up our own dog park. It was going to be a tedious, trying process, but necessary to remove the possibility that a dog might get away. It would also be less time consuming than walking each dog individually until each accomplished their respective "mission."

Amazingly, the dogs were the perfect traveling companions. They did not seem stressed at all, and relished the constant attention that the humans lavished on them. All of the volunteers were by definition dog lovers, and everyone who wasn't driving was petting.

Each dog found their favorite spot on a bed or bench and just slept the days away. Even during a monstrous thunderstorm just outside Vegas, they pretty much kept their cool, despite the fact that as California dogs they had very little experience with thunder.

I guess I shouldn't have been surprised. These dogs had been through the Los Angeles County shelter system and survived; there was no reason that a cushy ride cross-country, with good food and constant petting, should have upset them at all.

It should have provided a lesson for all of us in how to adapt and make the best of things, but that wasn't quite how I processed it. I found the whole thing to be a fairly miserable experience. I was working on almost no sleep, and I really mean working. There was plenty of physical labor, whether raising fencing or hauling dogs. Physical labor is not my favorite thing.

I was also worried about all the things that could go wrong, though very few things did. I had done part of the planning, and since I am keenly aware of my level of planning expertise, I had good reason to be worried.

The volunteers did seem to take their cues from the dogs, and they thoroughly enjoyed themselves. To this day, they (and

Debbie) describe the trip as one of the greatest experiences of their lives. I can only imagine that their lives to this point must not have been filled with great experiences.

But if the dogs didn't teach me anything, the humans did. Coming with us for a week like they did, enduring all of the hardships for people they mostly did not even know, taking all that time out of their lives for no personal benefit . . . all of that constituted incredibly generous acts. They were truly selfless and remarkable.

And what they did taught me a valuable lesson.

Never volunteer for anything.

All the dogs taught me . . .

about unwanted visitors.

When you have thirty or so dogs, you really can't have neighbors, or at least you can't have neighbors who like you. For this reason, we've always tried to live in houses that are pretty much in the middle of nowhere. Not that we have a choice; no self-respecting city in the middle of "somewhere" would let us live there.

So we wind up living in very rural, usually wooded areas. This was true of our house in Orange County, California, and especially of our house in Maine. They are both very beautiful areas, but quite isolated. At least in terms of humans.

Animals, not so much.

And we have all kinds of animals here . . . wild turkeys, red foxes, deer, bears, and a bunch of others that I haven't been able to identify. One thing is for sure; I know nothing about any of them.

That lack of knowledge, and my frustrating inability to conceal it, led to a rather public humiliation a few months after we moved in. I was having breakfast at one of our favorite local restaurants, Damariscotta Lake Farm, in Jefferson. It's a very friendly, neighborhood kind of place, where everyone knows everyone else.

The proprietor, Pete Souza, had quickly become a friend, and on this particular day he was taking the time to answer my questions about hunting. Deer hunting season had just started, and although it is not something I would ever do, I was interested to learn about it.

He explained to me that during any single season, state law dictates that a hunter is allowed to shoot only one deer, and it must be a male. Once that's been accomplished, the hunter can apply for a special permit, which will allow him to shoot a female.

This puzzled me, and I was foolish enough to reveal my confusion. "At a distance," I asked, "how can a hunter tell if it's a male or a female?" I was envisioning the hunter having to sneak under the deer to view its private parts.

Within three minutes, Pete revealed to everyone in the place that the idiot from the city didn't know that male deer have antlers, while females don't. I was the laughingstock of the place, and I was sort of indignant about it.

After all, I hadn't grown up with deer in Paterson, New Jersey, nor had I lived with them on the Upper West Side of Manhattan. "I'll bet there's not a person here who knows which subway to take to Coney Island" was my lame rebuttal.

It was especially lame because I don't have any idea which subway to take to Coney Island.

Then, to further my claim that no one from my type of background would know the intricacies of deer sexuality, or for that matter care about it, I said that when I got home I would ask Debbie, and she wouldn't know, either. That would somehow vindicate me.

So I left and went home, and as I'm telling Debbie the story, she immediately interrupted and said, "Male deer have antlers," and then proceeded to mock me in the same manner as the people in the restaurant.

And that's when I really blew it. "I don't understand," I said. "How does a female manage to give birth to a male with antlers?" I guess I envisioned deer doctors yelling "Push! Push!" to the mother in labor, and that mother screaming, "I can't! The damned antlers hurt too much!"

For two reasons, Debbie didn't even take the time to explain that the antlers grow later on. First of all, she was laughing too hard. Second, she was rushing down to the restaurant to tell everyone the even dumber thing that I had just said.

Despite all that, I don't hold a grudge, at least not against the deer. I really like them, and we feed the ones on our property all winter. But there are other animals I'm less fond of, and I would say that for the most part my fear of living things is in inverse proportion to size. Dog and cat, and above, no problem. I love horses and think deer are beautiful and majestic, even if I'm unclear about their sex. I'm fine around goats and cows. I'll pet them, touch them, and feel comfortable around them.

But when they get smaller, that's when I've got a problem. On our property we've seen possums, porcupines, wild turkeys, snapping turtles, and a whole bunch of rodents, and I wouldn't get near any of them. My problems also include birds, bats, and bugs of all shapes and sizes. We encountered flying insects in our house in California that could carry off Volkswagens.

I don't like to touch any of these things, and that means dead or alive. That wouldn't be such a problem if Debbie wasn't just as averse. In California one day there was a dead animal on our back porch, right at the entrance to our house. I think it was a possum, but I don't know how it died; most likely it wandered up, saw the dogs, and committed suicide.

The doors to the porch were always open so that our dogs could go in and out. Since they were in the center of the house, Debbie and I walked by them frequently, meaning we were within a few feet of the dead animal. For an hour, she and I pretended not to see it; I would whistle nonchalantly as I went by.

Needless to say, I caved, for two reasons. First of all, I knew that Debbie would outlast me; the possum could be there so long it mummified and she wouldn't touch it. Second, I was afraid that the dogs would eventually consider it a chew toy, and make it far more disgusting.

So I did what I always do in these horrible situations; I covered it with a towel, and then another, and then another. That way the towel coverings were so thick that when I scooped the animal up, I wouldn't actually be able to feel its shape. Of course, it meant throwing out the three towels along with the animal, but that was a small price to pay.

We had rattlesnakes on our property in California, and two of our dogs got bitten. My technique for getting rid of them was to call one of our neighbors, who would cut their heads off with a shovel. Of course, that's what they told me, and I believed them, but I never hung around long enough to see the act. If I were going to touch a snake with a shovel, the handle would have to be a quarter mile long.

The one time my neighbors weren't around, we found a rattlesnake in the driveway. I couldn't just leave it there, because it could have bitten one of the dogs. So I drove over it with my SUV, and the first time I did it, the snake didn't die, it just got pissed off. It took a second drive-over to finally kill it.

Our open-door policy in California, while necessary for the dogs to go in and out, brought numerous unwanted visitors. One time a pigeon flew in, and had no idea how to get out. The dogs were going insane, and the bird didn't seem to realize that it needed to stay high and out of their reach. It kept landing on the floor, then flying up to the mantel and other furniture.

I had no idea how to catch a bird, and no desire to do so, but I couldn't let the dogs kill it. The house had come with an outdoor hot tub, which we had gotten rid of, but in our garage was the pole and net that was used to scoop things out of the water. It was like an enormous badminton racquet.

I started chasing the bird around the house, wielding that thing. It was ridiculous; even if the bird had wanted to intentionally get into the net it wouldn't have been able to; the thing just wasn't practical for bird catching.

Debbie, with a burst of uncharacteristic courage, grabbed the pigeon with her hands. We had an outdoor, fenced bird sanctuary, and she put it in there with some new friends. The pigeon had a green band on its leg, so I figured it must be owned by someone and I hoped to return it.

I called a friend at an animal shelter who knows a lot about birds, and she said that it was a homing pigeon that had gotten lost. The fact that it lost its way meant that the owner would no longer want it or consider it useful. So the bird lived out its days in our sanctuary, and I'm sure regaled the other occupants with stories of the nuthouse that the humans lived in.

In Maine, the locals proudly claim that while there is a lot of weird stuff in the woods, there is nothing poisonous, not even the snakes or spiders. That is certainly a positive, but it doesn't quite make up for the fact that there is a disgusting array of things to deal with.

From our second-floor bedroom the other day, Debbie looked down and saw something dead midway up the stairs. She was positive that she saw wings, and that it was a bat. Her assumption was that one of the dogs either killed it or found it dead, and brought it in as a trophy. She dropped a towel on it.

I was out, and she broke the horrifying news to me when I got home. I would rather a serial killer entered our house than a bat, but once again I was called upon to be the man of the house, a task I am not well suited for. So I grabbed the obligatory two additional towels and did the scoop, tossing the towels and likely bat into the Dumpster.

My secret wish is that we could live in a sterile environment, maybe a biosphere. It would be a world free of bugs and snakes and rodents. It might be a boring existence, but one thing would certainly be true.

We'd save a hell of a lot of money on towels.

All the dogs taught me . . .

to respect (nonhuman) life.

We have a wonderful local theater in Damariscotta called the Lincoln Theater. The person who runs it, Andrew Fenniman, brings in the best movies, selected live performances, and live theater from Broadway and London. He has almost single-handedly turned our little town into a place with a rich cultural life.

We've seen a number of National Theatre of England presentations there, and recently we went to a showing of *War Horse*, beamed directly from London. Neither Debbie nor I had seen it on Broadway, nor had we seen the movie.

So the show started, and it was only a few moments before the horse made its first appearance. Except it wasn't a horse, it was just a collection of metal pieces put together roughly in the shape of a horse. There was no skin covering the metal, so it basically looked nothing whatsoever like a horse.

Just in case anyone could have confused it with an actual living metal horse, there were three men who moved it around, serving as its puppeteers. They dragged the hunk of metal to various positions on the stage, pretending to make horse movements and sounds.

Ten minutes in, one of the other characters got annoyed with something the fake metal horse did, and he smacked it. Not with a whip or anything, more like with a cloth. And he didn't hit it that hard; even a real horse wouldn't have been hurt by the smack. The metal horse, it should be said, didn't bat a fake horse eye.

A nanosecond after the slap, Debbie leaned over to me and said, "Let's get out of here." Not waiting for my response, she stood and started to move toward the aisle. Of course we were in the middle of the row, so we had to crawl over about eight people to make it out. Most of them were our friends, and when they asked where we were going, I lamely muttered something about fake metal animal abuse.

Now, two things must be said in Debbie's defense. First, she had been leery of the show in the first place, for just this reason. Second, there was an NBA playoff game on that night, so she pretty much knew I'd be fine with leaving the show early. I would have been even more fine with not going in the first place. In fact, I would have happily set fire to the fake metal horse, if I thought it would have gotten me back to the NBA game.

But the overriding point is that Debbie will simply not see or read anything that includes injury or death to an animal.

Just the animal being in danger makes it a nonstarter. She wouldn't see *Turner and Hooch,* or *Old Yeller,* or *Homeward Bound,* or *Marley & Me,* or many, many others.

But humans biting the dust? No problem. *The Godfather? Schindler's List? Saving Private Ryan?* Bring them on.

If there's one thing I've learned through my writing and my time in rescue, it's that Debbie is not alone in this madness. It is widespread.

When I speak at rescue events I sometimes talk about one of the less-than-memorable TV movies I have written, *Deadly Isolation.* Without boring you with the plot, it concerns a scam artist/criminal who, to further his nefarious and deadly scheme, must get a certain woman to fall for him.

The woman lives in a remote location on the coast with her elderly golden retriever, and I describe one scene in the script where the bad guy, woman, and dog go out on her boat on the ocean. When she's not looking, he throws the dog in the water. Then, pretending that the dog fell in accidentally, he jumps into the water and heroically saves it, so as to get the woman to love him even more.

Brilliant stuff, huh?

Every time I tell this story to the rescue audience, there is a collective gasp when I recount that the guy throws the golden into the ocean. Yet they obviously must know that I'm not going to drown a golden retriever, even a fictional one. Had I said that the guy went out on the boat and threw the woman into the water, everyone would probably yawn.

My Andy Carpenter books, being murder mysteries, contain a lot of humans getting killed, and sometimes the body count gets pretty high. I have never, not once, received a complaint about it; people just accept that it goes with the territory.

But I have literally gotten thousands of e-mails over the years begging me never to let anything happen to Andy's Tara. They tell me that when they buy the book, they skim ahead to the end before reading it, so as to make sure that Tara's name is still there, and that nothing bad has happened to her along the way.

And I'm not just talking about her taking a bullet. They don't want her to die of natural causes, or feel ill, or get a hangnail. And the same holds true for any other canine characters that might make an appearance. I've taken great pains to assure everyone that Tara is going to outlive us all, and that any animal that is in one of my fictional books is safe.

Humans, not so much.

All the dogs taught me . . .

**whether all things really do or
do not happen for a reason.**

I hear it all the time; many people say that all things take
place for a reason. It's a way to reconcile bad things that
have happened, to have faith that it ultimately will be a seen
or unseen blessing in disguise. It isn't always said in a religious sense, more as just a feeling that things will ultimately
make sense, and that they will work out the way they should.
It is the natural order of things.

I don't claim to have a background that has given me particular insight into this question, and I certainly don't want to
get into a religious debate. But my time in rescue has educated
me to my satisfaction on the question of whether all things
happen for a reason.

They don't.

I was in the Baldwin Park shelter in Los Angeles County

one day, and saw a six-month-old chocolate lab. He looked like a pure breed, but there is no way to really be sure. The one thing about his appearance that was beyond question was that he looked sick.

We only rescued a handful of puppies back then, since they had by far the better chance of finding a home than did older dogs. Of course, not very many dogs of any age or type made it out of Baldwin Park, but we had to make choices, and we usually opted for those with the least chance.

But this dog was an obvious exception to our rule. Dogs do not get nursed back to health in shelters like this; they get put down. Disease spreads quickly in these places, and sick dogs were either put in quarantine where the public could not see them, or they were put down to avoid contagion. Either way, they wound up dead.

So we took the dog, named him Chuck, and brought him to the vet where we kept our rescue dogs. Our vet quickly determined that he wasn't just sick; he was very sick. He had parvo, a very contagious virus that is often deadly. It attacks the gastrointestinal system of dogs, causing vomiting, diarrhea, etc.

The vet put Chuck on intravenous fluids, antibiotics, and even gave him blood plasma transfusions, which is pretty much all you can do. Chuck was housed in the quarantine area, so as not to infect other dogs. His assessment was that Chuck would probably not make it; that the time in the shelter delayed his treatment to the point that our efforts would likely prove too little, too late. All we could do was maintain him, give him the best possible chance, and wait.

So nobody was giving up, least of all Chuck. We visited him frequently in the quarantine unit; Debbie would stop there on the way home from work every day. Often he looked terrible, as if the end was near. I arrived one time and he seemed completely unresponsive to the point that I thought he had died, and I ran to get the vet technician. He was still alive, but at a low point.

Other times he was doing great. He would stand up when we got there, tail wagging, putting his head right up to the bars so that we could pet him. We did so, though each time it necessitated a thorough scrubbing of our own hands and arms with soap and bleach, so that we couldn't spread the disease to the other dogs.

But one thing was for sure, Chuck was not a dog that was about to give up on life.

And then one day it was over. I showed up (fortunately it was not Debbie), and Chuck was lying on the floor unmoving. For a moment I thought he might be just having another bad day, but I was wrong.

It was his last day.

There is no reason that Chuck had to live the brief life that he lived. No reason that a wonderful, happy dog like that had to wind up in a shit hole of a shelter, no reason he had to get so sick, no reason he had to suffer like he did, and no reason he had to die.

No reason at all.

Just like there was no reason that Sonny, a golden mix with a disposition as upbeat as mine is downbeat, had to have his jaw wired shut so that he wouldn't bark. No reason that the wires cut into his face so severely that he had permanent marks on his nose and the underside of his chin.

No reason at all.

I could go on, with countless other examples of great dogs

that we knew that were horribly mistreated, but I won't. You no doubt get the drift by now, and you're probably like Debbie and don't want to hear it.

But I will say that there is no reason that almost four million dogs and cats get euthanized every year, unless you count as a reason the fact that humans are assholes.

Chuck could have had a great life. We would have adopted him out to a loving family, and as a puppy he could have lived with them for many years, going for swims, and eating biscuits, and going on walks. Someone would have doted on him, and he would have responded with love and loyalty. Someone would have carried his picture on their cell phone and shown it proudly.

And when it was time for Chuck's life to end, it would have happened humanely, in a vet's office, while being held by someone who had loved him for his entire, long life.

But none of that happened. Instead he suffered in a shelter, and then died in a cage.

For no good reason.

All the dogs taught me . . .

about the art of public and nonpublic speaking.

Prior to my transformation to dog lunatic, I had not had many occasions to speak publicly. I had been on some television programs for interviews about the movie business, and later on I was on the *Today Show* when *Bury the Lead* was named by Janet Evanovich as a Book of the Month.

But in terms of speaking to audiences, my appearances were few and far between. Just a few presentation speeches at movie industry functions, and then of course there was that humiliating debacle when I got emotional doing the reading in which Andy's father died at Yankee Stadium. But really not very much, and I wasn't terribly comfortable doing any of it.

That was then, this is now.

Now I probably give twenty-five to thirty speeches a year.

I have turned virtually all of my book signings into benefits for rescue groups around the country. The local group has a cocktail party or dinner; they charge admission and have a raffle and/or auction. Then I give a speech, after which I sign books brought in by a local bookstore. The store gives part of the proceeds to the rescue group.

In addition to raising much needed money for the rescue groups, it's also self-serving for me. Many more people turn out than would at a normal bookstore signing, so we sell far more books in these settings.

I talk about my time in Hollywood, then my work as a screenwriter and novelist. I think it's all charming and witty, and I amuse myself endlessly. Then I start talking about dog rescue and *Dogtripping*, and I can see everybody sit up in their seats.

When I finish and invite questions, the percentage of questions that are about dogs is somewhere in the area of one hundred. That is what the audience loves, and that is what they are there to hear about.

Afterward, almost everyone who approaches to get a book signed has their smartphones out, so that they can show me pictures of their own dogs. Then they ask me to sign the book to their dogs by name. Some of them are a little embarrassed about it, but they needn't be. I understand it, and I'm actually interested in seeing the photos.

I'm completely comfortable in these settings. They are almost all dog people, which means it's like I'm with family. I talk conversationally, because these people get what I'm saying, and know exactly where I'm coming from. Many of them don't even think I'm insane.

In fact, the only part that's a little weird is the praise I get for what I've done in dog rescue. The truth, as much as I hate to admit it, is that most of the people I'm talking to have done more than I will ever do; I just have a platform to shout from. They have dedicated their lives to it, while I am comparatively a doggy-come-lately. But they seem content to let me speak for them.

As smooth as my rescue experiences have made my public speechmaking, they haven't been as kind to my private conversations. That is because of *Dogtripping,* and the book you are reading right now will only increase the problem.

There is a *Seinfeld* episode in which the Kramer character is said to be a master storyteller, weaving eccentric yarns that make him very popular with friends. Then Elaine's boss, J. Peterman, decides that she should ghostwrite his autobiography. Since his own life doesn't seem quite interesting enough, he purchases Kramer's stories to use as his own. Kramer is then left with no stories to tell, since Peterman now owns them. He becomes frustrated by his inability to regale his friends with stories.

My situation is somewhat similar. My entire recent life is contained in these books, and most of my friends have read them. So almost every time I start to tell a story in conversation, I realize that they have heard them already.

Fortunately, I'm about 130 years old, so I lived for a long time before getting into rescue. My experiences back then weren't particularly interesting, but I'm a fiction writer, so I'm good at making things up.

If you knew me back in the day, and you meet any of my current friends, please don't mention that I wasn't really a war hero, flying hundreds of combat missions over enemy territory. And keep it to yourself that I wasn't a star quarterback, constantly fending off adoring coeds. Just nod if they say I got sixteen hundred on my SATs, and didn't sign with the football Giants only because I chose to become a Rhodes Scholar instead.

I get away with saying all that, because the truth is that once people realize that I in fact live with as many as forty large dogs, all the rest of that stuff seems comparatively believable.

Believable, not enviable.

All the dogs teach me . . .

how to multitask.

I admit it . . . I'm not the hardest worker in the world. I never have been. I worked long hours in the movie business, but only because I had to in order to get the job done. It did not come naturally to me.

Being a novelist requires a lot of self-discipline, and that is not something I have in large supply. You only have to read my books to know that I am not a slave to my writing, or especially to research.

I once wrote an entire Andy Carpenter book, called *Dead Center,* which took place in Northern Wisconsin, and the crime that was revealed at the end revolved around things being smuggled across the border from Canada.

I sent it to the publisher, and mentioned that while they

read it, I was going to check out a map to find out real town names near the Wisconsin-Canada border, and then substitute them for the fake names I had used.

The problem was that the map revealed one key fact that I had overlooked: Wisconsin doesn't share a border with Canada. So I had to rewrite the book, and the stuff had to be flown across Lake Superior. Which meant I had to make the bad guy a pilot, and put an airfield in the town.

Then I got creative and had one of the ways in which Andy solves the crime be that the bad guys never filed a flight plan. It was only after the book came out that I found out from e-mailing pilots that you don't have to file a flight plan.

And all of that could have been avoided if I had taken the time to look at a map in the first place.

So hard work isn't really my thing, and for most of my life, I haven't even liked to task, never mind multitask. Which is a major reason why it's fair to say that my current life hasn't exactly gone according to plan.

Today's a workday. I'm going to write this chapter, and maybe a few others. I don't know that many writers, but I imagine for most of them that means going into their office, turning on their computer, and diving into it. Total concentration; almost all writers will tell you that the craft demands it.

So far today I have cleaned up the yard, not a small or pleasant task. I've also cleaned up one or two spots where the dogs inexplicably didn't quite make it out to the yard. I've filled the water dishes three times, and we have eight water dishes.

I've "prepared" and "served" twenty-one meals, then picked up the dishes and washed them. I've given out medicine to thirteen dogs, including pills, liquid, and two antibiotic capsules to Mamie, who insists that they be housed in meatballs.

So now it's 9:00 A.M., and I'm ready to go. I'll be writing until ten thirty, at which point I have to take a black lab named Dallas to the vet to have a growth removed. The vet is forty-five minutes from our house; there are vets closer, but we're very particular and happy with Dr. Dan Dowling, the one we've chosen.

I should be home by twelve thirty, and then will write until two, at which point I'm going to Augusta to get dog food. That'll take a couple of hours, but I'll get at least two hundred fifty pounds of kibble, so we're good for nine or ten days. Loading it into the car and then carrying it into the house are two of my least favorite things to do.

It'll be afternoon feeding time when I get home, and I'll finish that by about five thirty. Then I've got the evening medicine to administer, after which I'll write again, although my hours will be limited by the fact that there's a Monday night football game tonight. I do have my priorities.

I've left out my human-related activities, such as meals. If you've gotten a look at me, you'll know that I don't miss too many of them, so that takes up some time.

Now, in fairness, I don't have some of the other chores that many other writers might be stuck with. I do absolutely nothing around the house, due to a combination of the aforementioned laziness and lack of ability. We literally have a handyman come to change our lightbulbs, mostly because it's easier not to have to function in the dark.

If anything mechanical goes wrong, Debbie doesn't even bother to tell me about it. That's because I have demonstrated that first I'll complain bitterly about having to try to fix it, and then my subsequent efforts will only make the problem worse.

She simply picks up the phone and calls the appropriate person, be it plumber, electrician, whatever. Not that I have no role to play; I help keep the dogs from going insane when they come to fix whatever was broken.

Probably the most difficult thing I have to do is just getting in and out of the house. Most people don't find that such a big deal; they just open the door and walk through it. I only wish it were that easy. What simple, carefree lives those people must live.

When Debbie or I open the door to leave, pretty much every dog in the house wants to go with us. So they mob the area, and we have to try to squeeze our way out, while at the same time preventing them from getting through. The task is complicated by the fact that right in front of the door is Bumper's sleeping place, and he requires his own water dish, which invariably gets dumped out in the process.

Getting back in is even harder. When we're leaving, we can sometimes do so quickly, without them realizing it's going to happen, thus utilizing the element of surprise. In our return maneuver, we lose that advantage. They are camped out at the windows, ready to pounce on us as we come in, all the while still trying to get through the open door.

There is simply no sneaking in without the dogs' window observers spotting us; they are vigilant and always alert. If Osama bin Laden had those kinds of sentries on duty when the Navy Seals arrived, he'd be doing terrorist talk shows today.

Strangely, if in the departure or arrival process any dogs actually manage to make it outside, they immediately want back in. They don't try to leave the porch, and actually look around, apparently bewildered. It's like they are saying "Hey, you're not playing the game . . . you're not supposed to let us out here." Then they go right up to the door and scratch at it.

It's apparently a scary world out there. Unfortunately, it's pretty scary in here as well.

All the dogs taught me . . .

you can't tell a dog by its color.

Almost everybody whose dog is a mixed breed will tell you with absolute certainty exactly what kind of mix it is. Shepherd/beagle. Lab/collie. Newfie/golden. Pomeranian/mastiff. Pomeranian/mastiff?

Their supposed knowledge usually comes from two factors, the look of the dog, and its personality traits. They've done the research, and they have decided just what breeds are in their dog.

The fact of the matter, of course, is that no one really has a clue. Unless they were there to witness conception, and that gets into a whole other area that I probably should avoid, then the average owner of a mutt actually has no idea what his dog has in him. In fact, even witnessing conception almost always would not provide much insight.

The point is that it's rare that a pure-breed golden retriever sneaks out of the house at night and picks up a pure-breed German shepherd at the corner bar. Or that a pure beagle goes on Match.com to get a date with a pure cocker spaniel. Overwhelmingly the parents of mixes are themselves mixes, as were their parents, and their parents' parents. By the time the most recent generation is born, the offspring are likely to be a mix of at least a dozen canine strains.

And it often doesn't even matter what the dog looks like. In running the Tara Foundation, we almost never rescue puppies. There are a lot of reasons for this, the main one being that puppies are the most adoptable out of shelters.

But one time we made a notable exception. We found a beautiful, reddish pure-breed golden retriever in the West L.A. shelter. The golden was in the late stages of a pregnancy, and a few days later, she gave birth to six puppies. There was no way we would leave the golden in the shelter, but we obviously wouldn't take her without the puppies she was nursing.

We rescued the golden, who we named Lila, and her six puppies, all of whom were adorable.

And jet black.

So we knew beyond any doubt that the puppies were a minimum of fifty percent golden, yet by sight no one would ever be able to guess that. No owner of these dogs, if not for the fact that we told them the circumstances, would have ever referred to them as golden mixes.

Just as looks don't tell the tale, neither does personality. Certain breeds are known to have certain behavioral characteristics, although in my experience that does not come close to being reliable. But once various mixes enter the picture, all bets are off. You simply cannot guess the type of mix by its personality.

Basically people refer to dogs in whatever way suits them. Shelters and other rescue groups used to do this to us all the time. One episode in California stands out. A woman living in the Mojave Desert was arrested when it was learned she had almost three hundred dogs and was completely incapable of caring for them.

The situation was horrible; there wasn't enough food for all the dogs, fights and disease were rampant. But once the woman was arrested, then rescue groups were allowed to go in and help as many dogs as they could. And to their everlasting credit, a large number of rescuers descended on the place.

We had more than thirty dogs in our house at the time, and didn't want any more. But we told one of the rescue groups involved in the operation that if there were any golden retrievers found, we would take them. We had made a posthumous promise to Tara that we would never turn down a golden.

Lo and behold, the rescuers reported that they found two of them, and I went to pick up the dogs after their removal from the location. It turned out that they were not close to being goldens. I have no idea what they were mixes of, but the fact that they had a few strands of golden-colored hair apparently gave the rescue people license to tell us that they were goldens.

Their names were Sally and Jack, and they had been terribly mistreated. We of course took them despite the fact that I look more like Kate Upton than they looked like golden retrievers. They proved to be wonderful dogs, and actually made it on the trip to Maine.

Sally died about a year after we arrived here, and Jack is still with us. He loves to go for walks, especially in the snow, but the next time that someone sees him and says "look, a golden retriever" will be the first.

By the way, there are now DNA tests available for dogs to determine what their mix consists of. For seventy-five to a hundred bucks, you can get some of the dog's saliva on a swab, send it in, and find out. We've never cared enough to use this service, but a lot of people, and a bunch of rescue groups, have done so. At best it is something for the curious, and not the kind of thing that should substantially influence any decisions.

Because all I can say is that the breed and type of mix are far less important than most people think. It's the individual dog that matters. Always.

Charlie taught me . . .

in rescue, the key is being able to *adapt*, not just *adopt*.

A little more than a year after Tara died, Debbie was still not emotionally ready to get another dog. Yet she loved them and wanted to be around them, so a friend recommended a possible solution . . . volunteer at an animal shelter.

We signed up at the West Los Angeles shelter, about ten minutes from our Santa Monica home. It was the best of the L.A. city shelters, which isn't saying much. Dogs were still put down there when they got overcrowded, but not to the degree that the euthanasias were taking place at the other shelters. The adoption rate was not particularly good, but again it was better than the others.

In addition to doing adoptions out of their facility off Bundy Avenue, the shelter would recruit staff and volunteers to do occasional mobile adoptions. This meant taking a group of the dogs to an outdoor mall, setting up signs, and hoping people would stop by, fall in love with a dog, and take it home. The theory was that we were going to the adopters, rather than waiting for the adopters to come to us.

I understood and appreciated the shelter's desire to be aggressive, but neither Debbie nor I have ever been fans of mobile adoptions, and we never did them once we started the Tara Foundation. Bringing a pet into a home should be a carefully thought out decision, and mobile adoptions encourage impulse purchases. The ultimate success rate for spur-of-the-moment adoptions is considerably lower than those that are planned, at least in my experience.

But despite our misgivings, we would volunteer for these sessions, mainly because a good number of the dogs otherwise had little chance to escape the shelter alive. So each of us volunteers would sit with a dog, and hope that people would come over and interact with it.

Often someone would come over and pet the dog, and tell me how cute it was, and just when I thought maybe they were going to adopt it, they'd tell me how they would take it in a heartbeat, if only their landlord would allow dogs. And when that conversation was over and they walked away, they would have no idea how close I came to strangling them.

Eventually, more than a year after Tara died, Debbie had gotten to where she was ready to get a dog of our own, a point I had reached long before. Fortuitously, a beautiful, three-year-old golden retriever was found stray, and brought into the shelter. They named him Skipper, and held him the required five days, to give his owner a chance to find and claim him. The chance to rescue a golden retriever was extraordinarily appealing to us, since that was and remains by far our favorite breed.

There was a mobile adoption on a Sunday, but Skipper was not going to be there. His five days weren't going to be up until Monday, and he would thus become available to the public on Monday morning. We had already made our decision; we'd be there when they opened to adopt Skipper and welcome him to our home.

The dog that Debbie sat with at this particular mobile adoption was named Charlie. The shelter referred to him as an Australian shepherd mix, but that was for lack of anything else to call him. He looked nothing like an Aussie shepherd, or like any other breed; he probably had a hundred different breeds in him.

Another thing he had was virtually no chance to get adopted, either at the mobile or the shelter. He was nine years old and more than ninety pounds, neither of which is likely to get a mixed breed to be sought after.

Charlie was incredibly sweet, and Debbie bonded with him, and did her best to convince potential adopters of his worth. But nobody came close to taking the bait, no matter how much she sang Charlie's praises.

As human volunteers at these mobile adoptions, we would feel a lot of pressure. We were powerless to force anyone to take a dog, but in the back, actually the front, of our minds was the knowledge that if the dogs weren't taken, and were brought back to the shelter, their lives were in major danger. We'd find ourselves watching the clock and dreading the end of the day, because that would mean failure. And not to be too dramatic about it, but failure more often than not meant death.

So Charlie did not get adopted that day, and we took him back to the shelter with the other dogs. Locking him back in his cage was a very difficult thing to do, which is probably why Debbie had me do it. The whole thing was very, very depressing.

The next morning we were there before the shelter doors even opened to get Skipper, who happened to be in the dog run next to Charlie. We waited near the entrance, in the parking lot.

Another woman was waiting there as well; her name was Denise, and she told us she lived in Redlands, about an hour east of Los Angeles. She had been made aware of Skipper's arrival at the shelter when he was first brought in, and had visited him three times in the last five days. She was beyond excited at the prospect of adopting him, and had brought with her a bag full of toys and biscuits for him. She also showed us photos of her previous golden, who had died six months before, and it was clear from the photos that he had been a deeply loved dog.

The way it works at the shelter is that if more than one potential adopter shows up when the dog first becomes available, an auction is held, and the person that is willing to pay the most gets him. It rarely happens other than in selected situations where a beautiful and young pure breed is involved. Of course, Skipper qualified on both counts.

Denise was a little worried about this, because she was not a woman of means. She had no idea that we were more than just volunteers at the shelter, or that we were going to be her opposition in the Skipper auction. It was clear to us from the way she was talking that we could outbid her for Skipper, and we planned to do so.

I'm sure you've known where this is going for quite a few paragraphs now. We entered the shelter, and there was Charlie, and there was Skipper, and seeing the two of them made our decision for us. By not insisting on the golden, by adapting to the circumstances, we were able to get two great dogs in terrific homes.

Charlie came home with us, and Skipper went home with Denise. She didn't have to bid for him, since there was no one to bid against. And we certainly didn't have to enter an auction for Charlie, we were his only suitors. Both dogs walked out of there with their heads held high, and Charlie sat on Debbie's lap the whole way home.

So Charlie was our first rescue, and was right up there with our best. Hanging proudly in my office, framed by Debbie, is the check for twenty-two dollars and fifty cents, made out to Los Angeles County Animal Control, which we used to buy Charlie's freedom. It was money very well spent.

We had Charlie for three years, until he contracted cancer and died. He was an only dog for just a couple of weeks, after which we started bringing friends home to live with him. One after another, after another, after another . . .

He welcomed them with open paws, seemingly happy to share the spotlight. I think Charlie was grateful to us for bringing him into our family, and we were grateful to him for teaching us what rescue is all about.

Charlie remains one of our all-time favorite dogs, and I believe he was very happy living with us. I hope Skipper was just as happy with the woman from Redlands.

Wanda taught me . . .

**the casual choices we make
mean *everything*.**

Back in the seventies, I had a friend and writing partner named David Marlow, who at the time had the job of story editor for United Artists.

We met when I got a freelance job working for him. I would read scripts that had been submitted and write a synopsis and an opinion on whether they should be made into a movie. To give you an example of how good I was at that, I gave a thumbs-down on *Carrie*.

David told me about a book his friend had written, which at least at the time had never been published. I might have the details of the story slightly wrong, since it's been a very long time, but the gist of the theme certainly remains intact.

The story concerned a guy who lived on the Upper West Side of Manhattan. He was heading downtown, and had three modes of transportation available to him. He could take a bus, hail a cab, or walk. It was not exactly a momentous decision.

He decided to take a bus, and during the ride met a woman he had known and dated in high school. They reconnected, started to date, fell in love, and married. He went into her father's business, which then unraveled in fraud. He became implicated in it, and with his life falling apart and facing jail, on page 150 he committed suicide.

Then the reader turns the page, and the guy decides to take a cab downtown instead, so he doesn't meet the woman on the bus, and he winds up living a completely different life. Then on page 300, he decides to walk, and a third life unfolds.

The obvious point, which is also brilliantly illustrated in the Broadway show *If/Then*, is that the little, seemingly incidental choices that we make can change everything. Whether you believe it's fate, or just the power of the arbitrary, we take paths for reasons that are apparently accidental, but have huge impact.

When I was in Houston for a book signing, Debbie got the call to go to the East Valley shelter to rescue Mamie, a nine-year-old golden that was to be put down. While there she did what she always did, she checked out the other available dogs, and wound up with a black lab and border collie mix as well.

She used the restroom near the back of the shelter, and then headed back to the main office to finish the adoptions. Being unfamiliar with that shelter, she made an incorrect turn and walked down the wrong aisle, through the area where unavailable dogs were housed.

It was in one of the unavailable cages that she saw Wanda,

an obviously abused mastiff who weighed only 105 pounds. Every rib on Wanda's frame was visible; she had been starved and mistreated. She was not in the public viewing area because she had only been there for four days, and would not be up for adoption until the fifth.

Had Debbie not walked down the wrong aisle, she would not have seen Wanda, and I would not have gone back the next day to adopt her.

Of course, there is no way to know what would have happened to Wanda had we not gotten her. Most likely she would have been euthanized; that would certainly not have been an unusual event at that shelter. Or maybe she would have been adopted, and because of her massive frame been used as a guard dog, patrolling an area behind a fence all day, without the human contact she so clearly craves.

But I'll tell you one outcome that would have been as unlikely as a Mets World Series victory next year. And that is that Wanda would be adopted into a welcoming home, would put seventy-five extra pounds on her frame, would be surrounded by dog friends for her to play with, and would sleep in a bed every night with humans who love her.

In rescue unhappy outcomes happen all the time, because there are so many more deserving animals than there are homes for them. When the Tara Foundation was at its peak, we would go to a shelter every week, and fill up all our available spots, replacing those that had gotten placed in homes the previous week.

Between L.A. County and the city shelters, we had at least ten shelters we could have gone to. Usually the decision concerning which one to go to each week was made for reasons having nothing to do with the dogs; perhaps we had to run another errand nearby one.

So if we went to the Downey shelter, then maybe ten dogs housed there lived, when they would otherwise have died. And if instead we went to Baldwin Park, then ten from there would have made it out. And the worst part is, of course, the reverse. Wherever we didn't go, then those dogs that could have been saved, were not.

It's arbitrary, and it's unfair, but it's rescue.

Mugsy and Little Sarah taught me . . .

that size really doesn't matter.

Of the hundreds of dogs we've had in our house, I can only remember two that were less than fifty pounds. The average is probably closer to eighty or ninety, and we've had many one-hundred-pounders and above. But the two "runts of the litter" were Mugsy and Little Sarah.

Mugsy was probably thirty pounds, and at that he was sort of stocky on his little frame. He had a Chihuahua look about him, though he was considerably larger, and had short, tan hair. He also had one eye; the other had apparently been removed surgically, and the socket sewn closed. The remaining eye was quite large, making him look like a Chihuahua/cyclops mix.

The other thing he had was an attitude, and it might be that attitude that attracted Debbie in the first place. She saw him in the Seacca shelter in Downey; he was one of five dogs in the overcrowded run, and all the others were twice his size. But none of them were messing with him, that's for sure. Mugsy had swagger.

We simply never took a dog Mugsy's size, but Debbie just had an instinct to get him out of there. He was nine years old, and not the best-looking dog in the world, and he had the one eye, so not only did we know that he'd never get adopted from the shelter, but we also knew that we'd have a hard time placing him ourselves. Because of that, we didn't put him up for adoption, we just brought him home.

It was really a test, and I was more worried about it than Debbie was. I was afraid Mugsy couldn't handle himself surrounded by thirty or so other dogs, the smallest of which was literally twice his size. I was worried about whether or not he could survive in our environment, and if he couldn't, we'd obviously have to put him up for adoption. He would have been very tough to place, and I didn't want him to languish in a cage.

But he did more than survive.

He dominated.

The other small dog we had was Little Sarah, a beagle, about thirty-five pounds. We were in the Orange County shelter, rescuing a chocolate lab named Hershey, when Debbie saw her in a run. The sign on the door identified her as being ten years old, and revealed that her owner had voluntarily relinquished her.

No reason was given for turning her in, but it wouldn't matter anyway. People who left their dogs at a shelter were completely unreliable as to the reason. Some would say negative things about the dog so as not to look bad for dumping it.

Others might say overly nice things about the dog in the hope of increasing its subsequent chances of adoption.

Generally, friendly dogs come up to the bars of the cage when humans come by and pay attention to them. Not Sarah. They had set up a dog bed and water dish for her in the back of the run, and that's where Sarah stayed. She sat there like a queen, regally surveying all who came before her, but not deigning to grant them an audience. Already she was dictating terms.

So Debbie took her. It just bugged her that a ten-year-old dog, with the obvious dignity that she had, should have been dumped in that place by an idiot owner. We decided we'd call her Little Sarah, because we already had a Bernese mountain dog named Sarah at home.

We loaded Little Sarah and the hundred-pound Hershey into the backseat of our car, and watched as Little Sarah snapped at him, and he backed off.

It was a foreshadower of things to come.

We did not have these two smallish dogs at the same time; Mugsy died about a year before we got Little Sarah. But they were cut from the same cloth. Mugsy had a more pleasant personality, but they each inspired fear and respect from their much larger brothers and sisters, and demonstrated no fear themselves.

Mugsy was tough as nails. When he was twelve he had severe kidney problems, and required fluids administered into his back every day. We did it, and it must have been painful, but he didn't blink an eye, even though he had only one to blink.

Yet he could also be gentle, and liked nothing better than to be lifted onto the bed, so he could snuggle. When Mugsy finally died, it was a simply terrible feeling. The world lost a great one that day.

If Mugsy ruled with a firm hand, Little Sarah did so with a closed fist. Except for Debbie, everyone was afraid of her, and I was certainly in that group. Dogs the size of Wanda and Bernie would walk clear around the house to avoid passing by her and possibly incurring her wrath. If she wasn't a beagle, and Mamie a golden, I would believe that they were blood relatives.

She also had a bark that was beyond belief. We could have thirty-five dogs barking at once in a deafening cacophony of sound, but Little Sarah could be heard above them all.

Little Sarah was the only dog ever to escape off our property, slipping through a small opening when the gardener neglected to fully close a door. We lived in a dangerous area for small dogs, or large ones, for that matter. It was heavily populated by rattlesnakes, coyotes and even, it was rumored, a mountain lion and a wildcat.

The knowledge that Little Sarah was out there for many hours was torture for us; even though we hadn't done anything wrong, we felt like we let her down. But we eventually found her, and she returned to the group head held high, not sharing details of her adventure, but making it obvious she was not intimidated by it. It's entirely possible she killed a mountain lion or two in the process.

Little Sarah survived long enough to make the trip to Maine, and lived here for a year before dying at the age of sixteen. While we had her she led a great life, and took no prisoners.

Of course, the flip side of small and tough is large and meek. We've had mastiffs, Newfie mixes, Bernese mountain dogs,

Great Pyrenees . . . all large and most of them scared of their own shadows. Maybe it's that their size alone made them fearsome and intimidating, so they didn't have to develop the attitude to go with it. But they avoided confrontation at all costs, and usually backed down when they couldn't avoid it.

Certainly there would have been no way you could get Wanda, at 175 pounds, to step into the ring with Little Sarah, at thirty-five pounds. To coin an old Muhammad Ali phrase, Little Sarah would have hit her with so many lefts, Wanda would be begging for a right.

I don't think Mugsy and Sara knew they were small, but if they did, they certainly didn't care.

Tara and our seniors have taught me . . .

there's nothing wrong with growing old.

They have had limited success. I'm not getting any younger, and sometimes that bothers me, and sometimes it doesn't. Here's an example of a time it bothered me:

Debbie and I were traveling back from New York, and we were at JFK. Debbie had broken her ankle, and she was in a wheelchair. So a member of the airline staff took her through security, past the line and down a lane off to the side.

I was going through regular security, and as I got on the other side of the metal detector, a TSA agent with a German shepherd came over to me. The dog was pretty much dragging him, and he started sniffing me intensely (the dog, not the agent).

I laughed and explained how many dog smells I must have

on me, but I don't think he quite believed me. "Have you been loading ammo?" he asked.

I shook my head and said, "There is no one on the planet less likely to have loaded ammo than me."

He told me to get my stuff, that they'd have to check my palms. I had been carrying Debbie's crutches, and they had gone through the screening machine. The agent pointed to them on the security conveyer belt, and said, "Are those yours?"

I shook my head. "No, they're my wife's."

He nodded and pointed to a woman nearby in a wheel-chair and said, "Is that her?"

It wasn't.

Nothing unusual about any of this, except for the fact that the woman in the wheelchair had to be one of the oldest living human beings on the planet. I'm pretty sure Willard Scott wished her a happy hundredth birthday on a *Today Show* segment . . . in 1987.

The chance that I might be married to her was substantially less than the chance I had spent the day loading ammo.

I wanted to scream, *"Are you out of your mind? You think we could be married? That woman was probably my father's third-grade teacher! How old do you think I am?"*

I didn't, of course, because I didn't want to embarrass the woman, or the TSA agent, or myself. But it did cause me a moment of concern over just how old I must look, or whether I walk stooped over, or whatever.

I don't feel old, and the move to Maine has sort of invig-orated me. I graduated from college very young, and was married at twenty, so I always had to behave older than my years. I sort of feel like the lyrics of the song by Bob Dylan apply to me: "I was so much older then, I'm younger than that now." But the chronological truth, much as I try not to focus on it, is that I really am a lot older now.

These days I live my life surrounded by canine seniors, and in many ways they are like their human cousins. The hair on the top of their head doesn't turn gray, that honor is left to the hair on their face. But they get arthritis, and they walk more slowly. They have less energy, and want to sleep more. They're more prone to ailments, and more set in their ways.

There was a line in a movie I worked on called *About Last Night*. A young Demi Moore is in her kitchen, struggling to clean pots and dishes in the sink, and she says to a friend, played by Elizabeth Perkins, "It's official. I have become my mother."

Well, I am officially becoming our dogs.

I'm not sure what age a dog has to be to be characterized as a "senior." I asked Debbie, and she thinks eight years old, so I'll go with that. Unfortunately, because goldens are so cancer prone, many of them don't reach that status. Tara, for example, lived to be nine, but that ninth year consisted solely of her battle with cancer, so it was not a fun one.

But she handled it with grace and acceptance, and that's been true of all of our seniors. Most of them mellow, and some get crankier, but all of them retain their dignity. Unlike we humans, they don't complain about missed opportunities, or unrequited romance, or the tunelessness of current popular music.

I won't say that they all live life to the fullest, but neither do they give up. We have rescued dogs that were sixteen years old, and usually with ailments that cause vets to give them as little as three months to live.

We always hesitate to do so, because coming into our house is stressful, and we don't think a dog at that stage of its life should have to readjust to the bizarre surroundings. But the alternative is to have a dog die before its time, in a shelter, and that's just not acceptable.

And it always seems to work out. One of our first rescues was a dog named Buddy, who had five months to live. He was in terrible shape, but the vet put him back together and we brought him home. He wasn't part of the wrestling team, but he would sit on his dog bed and smile at the antics of his new family. We never regretted saving him for a moment.

Then there was Wilson, a golden who spent his first twelve years of life chained up in a backyard. We had him for two years, and he sure as hell made the best of his newfound freedom.

Then Tessie, a golden tied up and left in front of the Downey shelter in the morning before they opened. The attached note described her as fifteen, and the owners said that they were going on vacation and didn't want to pay to board her, so the shelter should put her down.

Tessie lived to eighteen with us, and hopefully it was long enough to make her forget the assholes she had lived with all those years. I hope wherever they went on their vacation, they contracted dysentery, and there was no indoor plumbing.

Of course, the tough part is knowing when age or illness makes their life not worth living anymore. As I said before, we weigh factors like whether the dog is eating, whether they can get up on their own and walk around, etc.

Just the fact that an old dog might lie in one place all day isn't enough to say that it does not have enough quality of life to continue. In fact, if just lying in one spot for hour after hour was a reason to euthanize, I would never survive an NFL Sunday.

Hopefully we all get old, canines and humans alike, and it presents new challenges and often new opportunities.

Tara really never got the chance to experience most of the perks of seniorhood, but because of her we've seen to it that many others did. It is an extraordinarily rewarding thing to do, and though it's not for everyone, I do strongly recommend it.

And if you see me on the street, or at a signing, please reassure me that the TSA agent was out of his mind.

All the dogs have taught me . . .

**that relationships are weird and
very unpredictable.**

Trainers will say that multiple dogs in a home cause them to form a pack order, a hierarchy by which they resolve conflicts and keep order. There will always, they say, be an alpha dog.

While I'm sure that is usually true, it doesn't work that way in our house. Maybe it's because there is no sense designating a dog as alpha if we have more dogs than the twenty-four letters in the entire Greek alphabet. Bottom line, it seems as if we have so many that the dogs just throw up their paws and say, "The hell with it."

But what is really fascinating is to watch various relationships develop within the group. There are pairs, and cliques, and loners. The dynamics and specifics often change and evolve, and it's pretty difficult to anticipate how they will do so. But they usually manage just fine.

Sometimes the relationships have developed before the dogs even come to our house. Quite often a shelter or rescue group will have two dogs that were either found or turned in together. The group correctly does not want to split them up; rather they want to place them in the same home. But when the dogs are seniors and therefore harder to place even individually, getting someone to take two of them is extremely difficult.

We bring senior pairs in all the time, and sometimes keeping them together turns out to be important, and sometimes not. We once rescued two ten-year-old goldens that the rescue group had named Napoleon and Josephine. They were inseparable; they even went outside to go to the bathroom together.

In the house they both hung out in the living room, and we'd often find them asleep, with Napoleon's head resting on Josephine's back. They were fine with the other dogs as well, but with the others they never established nearly as close a friendship as they did with each other.

Hunter and Tudor turned out to be a completely different story. I was doing a signing in Phoenix, and the local golden rescue group brought me two ten-year-old brothers. They were together their entire lives, and looked identical to each other. The only way I knew which was Hunter and which was Tudor was by the bandanas that they wore with their names on them.

I brought them home to meet our dogs, who decided that they didn't much care for the bandana fashion statement. Within fifteen minutes they had removed them, and for the next three years we had no idea which one was Hunter and which was Tudor. So we called them Hunter-Tudor. It worked fine.

However, Hunter and Tudor had basically nothing to do with each other during the time they lived with us. One hung out in my office all day, and the other was in the bedroom. They were friendly dogs, and interacted with most of their new buddies, but strangely did not seek out each other in any way.

They died at the age of thirteen, within three days of each other. Saying that makes it sound like one died and the other passed away soon after of a broken heart, but I'm not even sure the survivor knew the first one had died. I don't know how he could have.

Jessie and Black Cody (we already had a golden named Cody when he arrived) are two black lab mixes who came in together from the Lincoln County shelter here in Maine. Cody is very docile, while Jessie is aggressive with the other dogs. They steer clear of Jessie, or risk getting into a tussle.

But Jessie and Black Cody are completely bonded. I give them two food dishes, and they eat together out of the same one, and then together they go on to the next one. None of the others would dare try and share Jessie's food, but he willingly lets Black Cody do so.

Since most of our dogs do not come in as pairs, they form relationships with their newfound friends. It comes in all shapes and sizes. Sometimes it might be a group of five, who gather in the morning for a pre-breakfast wrestling match. We have a small hill on the fenced-in portion of our property, and the wrestling group goes out there when it snows and plays king of the hill.

Basically, Debbie or I could tell you the closest friend for most, if not all, of our dogs. But by far the tightest friendship is between Benji and Otis. They are absolutely inseparable, and if I take one to the groomer or vet without the other, the remaining one cries until we return.

As you might expect, there are some personality clashes as well. Very few of the dogs like Simon, a light-colored retriever mix. He's the Eddie Haskell of the house, nice to Debbie and I, but when we're not watching he gets under the skin of his colleagues.

Simon and Bernie have a particular dislike for each other, but they are smart enough not to let it get too physical. When there is any kind of excitement or barking outburst in the house, Simon runs halfway up the steps, and Bernie takes a position on the ground floor, next to the railing.

They bark angrily at each other through the railing, both using it as protection. Bernie could easily run up the steps if he wanted, or Simon could come down, but then they'd have no excuse not to fight. Clearly, neither of them wants to risk that, which is lucky for Simon, since Bernie outweighs him by seventy pounds.

But as close as many of them are, one thing stands out. Almost every one of them, almost every dog we've ever had, prefers human contact.

They want to be petted, and they want to be loved.

Many of the dogs have taught me . . .

all about quirks.

A s I've mentioned, when it starts to get light out in the morning, the dogs decide that the day has begun. Jenny, who sleeps with her head on my pillow, usually sounds the alarm by barking.

It's as if all the others have been poised and waiting for her signal, and they begin to bark in unison. I then must get out of bed, go downstairs, and feed them. Debbie, bless her heart, wouldn't get out of bed that quickly if it were on fire. And of course, there's no way she would go all the way downstairs to get coffee, not with me already down there. So instead she calls out, "Java Boy! Java Boy!"—a signal for me to bring some upstairs to her. Dignity has never been my strong point.

But, again, I digress.

It is supremely annoying to get up so early to such a deafening barrage, but it happens every day. Actually, it's almost every day. If I am out of town, or if Debbie is out of town, they don't do it.

No barking.

Not a peep.

They let Debbie or I sleep as long as we want; instead of waking us at five thirty, we wake them at seven thirty or eight o'clock. They obviously prefer when either of us is alone. When I'm out of town and they let Debbie sleep, it's like they're saying to her, "You want some rest? You want to sleep in all the time? Then dump that loser; we'll let you sleep to your heart's content every day."

This change in the morning ritual is inexplicable, at least to me. But it's just one of many quirks that the dogs have, individually or as a group, that seem to make no sense.

Many of them revolve around food. Dogs that will voraciously eat their meals if I place them down in the kitchen, would rather starve to death than eat the same food from the same dish in the den. Black Cody will lie on a recliner, apparently asleep, during the feeding. Then, just before I'm going to pick up the empty dishes, he gets off the chair and looks at me in a silent demand to finally get his dinner. And that only happens at the evening feeding; in the morning he shares his food with Jessie. I have no idea why, but I always cave.

Red Cody handles mealtime differently, and far more annoyingly. Debbie had two significant injuries this past winter, a broken ankle and then a torn Achilles tendon. Both required surgery, and a great deal of bed rest. Red Cody would lie on the bench at the end of the bed all day long, keeping her company.

His positioning extended to feeding time, and I would have to bring the food upstairs. But he wouldn't get down to the floor to eat it, and he wouldn't accept it being placed on the bench. Instead I had to put it on the bed, and when I did, he deigned to walk across the railing and eat it there. When he finished, he returned to the bench, and it was up to me to come up and fetch the empty dish.

Even though Debbie has been better for quite a while, and no longer is confined to bed, Red Cody has decided he prefers the previous arrangement. So I literally feed him every meal upstairs in bed, even though he is alone up there. I resisted once and didn't do it, so he didn't eat. I then gave in, because he has more willpower than I do, by a good margin.

Then there is the spill-on-the-floor phenomenon. Sometimes the dogs don't seem very hungry; kibble is left over in some dishes, and no one shows any interest in it. However, if by accident I or one of the dogs knocks over the dish, spreading out the kibble all over the floor, they fall over themselves to finish it. For some reason, there is something amazingly appealing to them about food scattered on the floor, even if the same food in a dish doesn't interest them.

When it comes to medicine, seven of our most arthritic dogs are on a pain med called Metacam, which is a liquid. I squirt the individual doses onto half slices of bread. All the dogs love bread, so I cut up pieces to give all of them as treats, though only the seven pieces have the medicine on them.

Bernie, our cleverly named Bernese mountain dog, is one of the dogs on Metacam, and he loves bread. But of course that doesn't mean he'll willingly take it. I offer it to him, and he literally turns his head, disdainfully avoiding it. I do so about five times, but he shows no interest in it.

So I say, "Then forget it. You can't have it," or some other embarrassingly immature comment like that. I walk away, and go back to giving out the bread to others. Then, when I finally return to Bernie, he grabs at the bread and devours it.

We also have dogs that, like Tara before them, won't eat biscuits in front of us, yet inhale them when we walk away.

Bernie has another bizarre habit when it comes to drinking water. We have many water dishes in various areas of the house, and if I carried each of them individually to the sink and back, the walking would violate my strict no-exercise regimen. So what I do is fill up pitchers, and then carry them to the dishes. Each pitcher-full is good for at least two and a half empty water dishes.

The moment I pick up a pitcher, Bernie swings into action. He follows me to the dish and drinks the water as I'm pouring it, before it gets to the dish. He guzzles it while it is en route to the dish, as if he is drinking from a park fountain.

I have no idea why he does this, but he has a great time, and he seems completely unconcerned that in the process he sprays water all over the floor.

The weird quirks don't only involve food. Simon will simply not walk through one area of our living room, yet it is almost always uninhabited, so he should have nothing to fear. Even when it is the most direct way toward where he is going, he will walk around the entire house so as to avoid that area.

Steeler, the largest of our six black labs, sleeps on our bed by himself for a good part of the day. He is young, by our standards, and very athletic, so he can get on and off the bed very easily.

But once he gets up there, he pretends to be afraid to get off. He'll bark, endlessly if necessary, standing at the edge of the bed and looking down to the floor, as if he's on a fifth-floor landing.

So Debbie or I trudge upstairs to help the poor guy down. As soon as he sees us get to the top of the landing, he jumps off . . . no problem. Then, starting in the early evening, he sleeps in the bathroom directly in front of the toilet. He's a large dog and hard to move, so without being too indelicate, bathroom plans must be made well in advance.

Of course, it's a little silly for me to write about the small lunacies and quirks our dogs possess, without admitting that in choosing to live like this, Debbie and I are far nuttier than they are. To paraphrase the great Hyman Roth, "This is the business we have chosen."

Update: Bernie has come up with two new quirks, as if he's desperate to get them in before I finish the book. He recently started pissing in the house, rivers of it, and we took him to the vet. The vet took X-rays and did blood work, but couldn't find anything wrong. It was completely uncharacteristic of Bernie, who is well house-trained, so we consulted a neurologist, who was baffled as well.

It turned out that Bernie has decided he will not go through the doggie door into the three fenced acres of land that is his bathroom. I have no idea why, but I now have to walk him three or four times a day out in front of the house, where he has decided he is more comfortable. So at six o'clock in the morning, in the dead of winter, you can find me outside with Bernie.

Even more annoying is another new one. Rather than get on the bed at four in the morning, he now wants to spend the whole night up there. When I go up, he's lying on the floor, and no coaxing can get him to get up on the bed. The moment I get in and pull the covers over me, there he is, front paws on the bed, barking to be lifted on.

Rescue dogs have taught me . . .

that people are the best, and that people are the worst.

Nancy Sarnoff lives in an affluent Southern California city with her husband Al, an extraordinarily intelligent and successful retired businessman. Nancy had a fine career in her own right, and is now retired as well.

There is no question that they have the means to live a life of leisure, which is why it is so remarkable that Nancy can very often be found "shopping" in animal shelters as over-crowded and depressing as you can find anywhere.

Nancy runs Perfect Pet Rescue, and by that I mean she runs it in a completely hands-on fashion, getting the dogs out of the shelter, making sure they are well cared for, and then supervising and arranging every adoption. There is no doubt that hers is a labor of love, but make no mistake about it, it is definitely labor.

Nancy was our mentor in starting the Tara Foundation, and my daughter's first rescue dog came from her. She started in full-time rescue long before we did, and has continued doing adoptions long after we stopped. Nancy has done it for twenty years, an amazing number considering how easy it is to get burned out by the sheer volume and need. She has personally rescued and found homes for more than eleven thousand dogs.

That is a remarkable achievement, especially if you think of it in years. She takes in mostly very small dogs, and they live longer than large ones. So just for the sake of doing the math, let's say they ultimately live to an average of fifteen years old. And let's say the average dog she rescues is four. That means she is giving each one of them an average of eleven years of additional life.

So by my count, she has provided 121,000 years of happiness for dogs that probably had never known any. And I could add that she never has less than seven in her own home. Debbie and I are two of the very few people on Earth who would think that the Sarnoff home seems empty with only seven.

I couldn't possibly mention all the great rescue people I know around the country; if I tried I'd leave too many deserving people out. But Barry Jacobs is one I am particularly proud of.

Barry rescued a golden retriever named Sherlock from the Tara Foundation in the mid-nineties. Sherlock wound up living to the age of sixteen, and was loved and cared for as well as any dog in the history of dogs.

But Barry's experience led him to join a golden retriever rescue group, and he works tirelessly at it. He, and certainly the group he is a member of, have been responsible for saving a remarkable number of goldens.

Barry credits Debbie and I for inspiring him to get into rescue, though the real credit of course belongs to Sherlock.

If a senior golden retriever gets dumped in the shelter, I can get five e-mails about it, all from people who live nowhere near the poor dog. Such is the power of the Internet. Most of these dogs are nowhere near Maine, so what I do is refer the information to golden rescue people that I know in whatever area the dog is in.

Close to one hundred percent of the time my e-mailing is unnecessary. They already know about the dog, and have made plans to get it once it becomes available. It doesn't matter how old the dog is, or what condition it is in. These people are incredibly caring, and they are relentless. They are going to save every single golden that needs saving. And other breeds have people just as dedicated.

It is not overstating it to say that there is a war going on in this country, undeclared and in many quarters unnoticed. Thousands of people have mobilized to fight the abandonment and mistreatment of animals. They are in every state and virtually every community, and they give their time and their money and their energy to save as many animals as they can. I have met a lot of them by doing rescue benefits around the country, and they are remarkable.

Sports fans will always talk about how hard it is to hit a baseball, that if you only fail seven out of ten times you've hit .300, and you're considered a success. In rescue the percentage is often far lower, and the consequences far greater.

So these rescue people know that if they don't save a dog, then no one will. Believe me, it's a lot of pressure.

And then there is the other side in the battle. That side is manned by the idiots who treat their dogs like they are disposable, worthless possessions, and who dump them without giving it a second thought.

We finally decided to stop volunteering in the shelters and start our own foundation because of a man who came into the Baldwin Park shelter with his three kids, turning in their one-year-old lab mix. Shelter policy is to have the owner sign a paper acknowledging that the dog could be put to sleep after one hour. This is not a nice place.

Debbie and I then overheard the jerk talking with his kids about the dog, and realized that he had adopted it there ten months earlier as a puppy. It was no longer a cute little puppy, so they were getting rid of it, and then going into the kennels to adopt another puppy. What a happy family moment.

Debbie berated him in the lobby to the point that they didn't get the new dog, and we rescued the one they brought in. But it was a small victory. I have no doubt that the idiot and his kids came back and did so later after she was gone. And by now the kids have probably grown to be just as stupid and uncaring as the father they learned from.

And that clown is one of so many. The Lancaster shelter north of L.A. is always overcrowded from picking up dogs that have been thrown out of cars into the desert. Countless owners bring their old dogs into awful shelters every day, claiming falsely that they found them as strays. Then they drive off, having dumped their "problem" on someone else.

There's actually a third group of people in the equation, and though they come down squarely on the good side, there is a negative aspect to what they do. These are people that many rescue people refer to as "rescue Nazis," though that is admittedly an unfair and unkind term.

They run rescue groups that are so strict in their require-
ments, that it is very hard for even the best dog owners to qual-
ify. Every group has parameters that an adopter must meet,
such as a fence around the yard, a promise that the dog will
live and sleep in the house, etc.

Some rescue groups actually do home visits, while some do
not. We never did that for a couple of reasons. First of all, since
it was basically just Debbie and I, we never had the time. But
secondly, we felt it was the people that were important, not
their home. Some of the best dog owners we ever met lived in
very modest homes, while some of the worst lived in luxurious
ones.

We never even cared if the people had a yard, and we particularly liked when the dog would be living in an apartment.
We found that they got better exercise that way, because the
owner would have to physically take them out.

When dogs are left in a yard, they don't do calisthenics,
they lie down and go to sleep. Some of the best dog owners
I've ever found live in New York City, because they are more
involved in their dog's lives, and their exercise.

But some of the more strident groups create rules that are
very hard for potential adopters to live up to, and as a result
they don't get the dog. I'd rather a dog went to a loving home
with a five-foot fence around their yard, rather than demand
a six-foot fence and the dog stay in a dog run, unadopted.

Not that anything bad will happen to the dogs; the rescue
groups would never allow that. They care too much about
them. But their strict policy results in fewer and slower adoptions, which means they will have less openings to bring in
new dogs. I just feel that since there are far too few homes in

the first place for the available animals, disqualifying some of the good ones is counterproductive.

Looking at the big picture, I'd like to say the good guys are winning the war. In some communities they are, and in others they're not. But they are all people I'm fine being in the foxhole with.

Gus and Sky taught me . . .

**that we have discovered a miracle
cure for separation anxiety.**

In 2003 I got a call from a woman at the Pasadena shelter. It's one of the best shelters in Southern California, which is why we did not go there very often. There was little sense in our taking one of their dogs, when they had a good placement rate themselves. Better we should frequent the places that needed our help, and there was certainly no shortage of them.

The woman and I had spoken once before, when she had called and asked us to take a twelve-year-old epileptic golden named Yogi. They had been unable to place him because of his age and condition, both of which made him an ideal candidate for us. Our taking him led to a perfect result. He loved being surrounded by so many dog friends, and medication kept the seizures completely under control. Yogi lived seizure-free and happy to the ripe old golden age of fifteen.

This time she was calling about two dogs, who they had named Louis and Gus. The dogs had been found stray, but together, and it was clear to the shelter people that they had come from the same home. They had assumed an owner would come and claim them, because the dogs seemed well cared for. But no one showed up, and the dogs were placed up for adoption.

The shelter decided correctly that they should be placed together, and they were. They went to a dog-loving couple, who had no children, and it seemed like a great match. Unfortunately, the first time the people went out, leaving Louis and Gus alone, Gus freaked out and went through a glass window, badly cutting his face.

Separation anxiety is a fairly common problem with dogs; they just become anxiety ridden when their owners leave. They can become destructive, and their attempts at escape can often lead to injury, sometimes serious. Such was the case with Gus.

The people consulted trainers, and tried a number of recommended solutions. Sometimes those solutions could involve leaving music or a television on, or leaving a piece of clothing with the owner's scent with the dog, or crating him. More severe cases sometimes call for tranquilizers. I'm not sure exactly what Gus's new owners tried, but they came to the conclusion that there was nothing they could do to resolve his separation anxiety, and finally in exasperation they returned both dogs to the shelter.

Enter us, and after getting the phone call, Debbie and I went down to meet them. Going to "meet" a dog in a shelter for us means going to rescue it; I cannot remember a single time in all our years of doing it when that wasn't the case. We view going there as a commitment, and the dog would have to carry a machete and draw swastikas in his cage for us to renege on that commitment.

When we got there we found exactly what the shelter worker had described, two beautiful goldens. Gus was a nine-year-old blonde, burly with a square-ish head. Louis looked just like Tara. Exactly and eerily like Tara.

So we brought them home and introduced them to their twenty-nine new friends. The introduction went well, as it usually does. Louis and Gus seemed comfortable, so after twenty-four hours of hanging out with them, we ran a test. We would go out for a short period of time, but not really leave. We'd just be out of sight near the house, listening for any kind of freak-out by Gus.

Nothing happened.

We extended the tests, leaving for longer and longer periods of time, but Gus showed no anxiety at all. This dog that had gone through a window when left alone with Louis, had no reaction at all when left alone with the mob.

Gus probably figured that separation anxiety was silly when he was so unseparated from so many dogs. Or maybe he was afraid the other dogs would make fun of him, or call him crazy. But if you have thirty friends to play with, how can you be upset and lonely when you're left "alone" with them?

We felt a little stupid; here we were hiding outside for an hour, only to return and find Gus resting comfortably on the couch. He didn't even have the courtesy to greet us at the door.

Meanwhile, it was clear that Louis was the perfect dog, a

fact that it turned out had obviously been recognized by the shelter. A few days after we adopted them, the woman from the shelter called again, to tell me a mistake had been made.

The executive director of the shelter had wanted to adopt Louis for his own home, but hadn't conveyed that fact to the woman who called me. So she rather sheepishly said that they wanted us to return him. We could keep Gus; the director didn't want him. So obviously their commitment to place them both together was not so great that they would refuse the executive director.

Fortunately, the request was made in a phone call with me, not Debbie. I turned them down, of course, but Debbie would have done so with a tad more fervor, and probably more colorful language. I told the woman that I would be happy to tell the executive director myself why he couldn't have Louis, if he wanted to call me. He didn't.

Louis, by the way, lived to make the trip to Maine, and just died last year. He was in the top three of the greatest dogs we've ever had, and Debbie truly believed he was Tara's descendant. Certainly, he was as devoted to her as Tara was.

In his last year, when it was hard for him to get around, he would nevertheless make it up the stairs to the bedroom to be near Debbie as she slept. He would be gasping for air from the effort, and I would help him by gently pushing him from behind, but there was no stopping him.

Then, in his last few weeks, when he simply could no longer navigate the steps, Debbie slept downstairs with him, on the couch.

Also, amazingly, in twelve years Louis never barked. Not even once. None of his colleagues could say the same, believe me.

Sky, a beautiful white shepherd, represented another example of our miracle cure. Sky was certifiably nuts, and was said to have an extreme case of separation anxiety. The rescue group was so concerned about it that they didn't want us to take him until there was a time that either Debbie or I would be home for at least the first three days after his arrival.

The person who turned Sky over to me was so worried that she literally spoke for fifteen minutes about her concerns. That fifteen minutes was about twelve minutes longer than it wound up taking for Sky to get comfortable living with us. He took one look at our house and its inhabitants, decided "yeah, this should work for me," and jumped on the couch.

Sky remained nuts through most of his long life, but he wasn't crazy enough to want to leave, whether Debbie and I were home or not. Crazy yes, stupid no.

Sky became a very sociable dog, both with his canine friends and with Debbie and me. He took a somewhat dimmer view of gardeners and FedEx drivers and visitors to the house, but we dealt with that, by keeping him away from them. Strangely, when we took Sky to the vet he became a pussycat, and all the employees there loved him. It was our house that he was protecting; once out of that environment he became friendly.

So be it Sky, or Gus, or any one of many other dogs that were predicted to be a problem, we never had any difficulty. All were very content with their surroundings and company, once they got to our house.

In fact, in all the years we've been doing this, the only one crazed and desperate to get out of our house has been me.

Tara taught me . . .

memories have meaning, and they live on.

I've already told the story of Tara's death a little bit in this book and in much more detail in *Dogtripping*, and I'll spare you a lengthy repeat here. I've talked about how we tried to avoid it, probably letting her linger too long, and how devastating it was for Debbie and me when it finally happened. And I've discussed how the period of time from her diagnosis to death was a transforming experience that quite literally changed our lives, and dictated the direction we would take.

But Tara's legacy is something I've only touched on briefly, and the sheer breadth of it is honestly amazing to me.

It really wasn't anything we consciously planned. The extent of our initial tribute to Tara was a small but significant way in which we decided to honor her. She always loved hot dogs, and would go crazy when we would grill them. Most times we would grill something else, usually chicken or fish, but we'd throw a couple of hot dogs on for Tara.

And in the last few weeks of her life, when she had lost most of her appetite, her love for hot dogs remained. So that's what we fed her, as much as she would eat. And when finally she refused even them, that's when we could no longer deny that her time had come.

So the small honor was that we would never eat a hot dog again, a vow we have now kept for twenty-two years. It's more of a sacrifice for me than Debbie, since she was never that crazy about them anyway. Had we sworn off broccoli or Brussels sprouts, the roles would be reversed.

That was it . . . that was all that was ever actually planned.

But primarily because of Tara, our love for dogs was such that we set about helping them by volunteering in shelters. And when that wasn't enough, we started a foundation, in her name, and we saved four thousand dogs.

Based on our e-mails, letters, and phone calls from people who have adopted from us, the experience convinced many that rescue was the way to go. I'm sure that when the dogs they got from us passed on they rescued again. So between the original four thousand, and however many more followed, the foundation work has been a hell of a lot more impactful than not eating a bunch of hot dogs.

And then came the Andy Carpenter books. In the first book, *Open and Shut,* I created Andy as a guy who was head over heels in love with his golden retriever. I gave her the name Tara, which wasn't that hard a name to come up with.

And because the person who first said "write what you know" definitely knew what he or she was talking about, in the second book, *First Degree,* I had Andy start a dog-rescue foundation. I really stretched myself creatively and came up with a name for it, the Tara Foundation.

So since then (and *Who Let the Dog Out?*, the thirteenth book in the ongoing series) Andy and Willie Miller have run the Tara Foundation and rescued dogs. And although the last thing I tried to do with those books is teach any kind of lesson, or deliver any messages, I wouldn't have minded it if a few people decided to rescue dogs because of them. Based on my e-mails, more than a few have, which is very gratifying.

If you analyze the plots to those books, there are often dogs involved, but not really in a crucial sense. Usually something happens with a dog that brings Andy into the case, but then the humans basically take over.

Yet, in reviews and comments and e-mails, people often refer to them as the "Tara books," or the "Andy and Tara books." Debbie and I sort of get a kick out of it.

So the legacy of Tara is that she has saved thousands of dogs, and she has gone on to secure her place in pedestrian American literature. Her name is probably known by a hell of a lot more people than mine. We have really honored her and given her a legacy way beyond what we ever intended or thought possible.

It makes me want to raise a beer glass and toast her, and then top it off with a hot dog.

Weasel and others taught me . . .

the importance of overcoming fears.

The truth is that Weasel only survived because she looked so damn scared.

We saw her in the Seacca shelter in Downey. It was the most unpleasant shelter to be in, because it was entirely indoors, with no fresh air. Other shelters had dog runs that were half inside and half outside, and not having that made the smell at Seacca close to unbearable.

We went there because there was so little chance for the dogs housed there to be adopted, and because a terrific guy named Ron Edwards ran the place. He cared deeply for the dogs, and because of that he instituted policies that made it easy for rescue groups to function.

Weasel was in a disgustingly filthy run with four other dogs, all bigger than her. She was pressed against the side of the run, and it took only one look at her body language, and especially her eyes, to know that she was petrified and miserable.

She was about fifty pounds and a year and a half old, which made her smaller and younger than the dogs we generally took for the foundation. But her fear, and our desire to relieve her of that fear, was the reason we took her.

We named her Ellie and brought her to the vet where we housed our rescue dogs, where they got a bath, medical care and shots, and from where they were adopted. But Ellie wasn't ready for a family; she was just too scared. She wouldn't let any potential adopters near her, wouldn't even go for a walk on a leash. She trusted no one, an attitude that was probably quite reasonable and justified, based on her life experiences to that point.

It took a month before she came around enough to be placed, and because she was young and cute, she was adopted right away. A woman took her as well as another dog, which we were happy about because we felt that a second dog might make Ellie more comfortable.

It didn't quite work out that way.

The woman took her two new dogs for a walk that first night, but accidentally left the door open slightly as she was bringing them back into the house. Ellie was out of there in a flash, and it was three days later that we found her shaking with fear in the West L.A. shelter, still wearing her leash. She was then, and remains, the only dog we ever rescued from a shelter twice.

Not wanting to put her through any more trauma, we took her home. We changed her name to Weasel, because she sort of looked like one, and she was just as scared in our house as she was anywhere else. When I put her on the bed with Debbie, she pissed on it. Debbie was understanding, because Weasel was so scared, and because Debbie is an understanding person, but mostly because it was my side of the bed that Weasel pissed on.

So we did what we always do in situations like this; we left her alone. We didn't try to socialize her, we didn't try to train her, and we didn't try to cajole her into mingling by giving her treats. We just left her alone, to assimilate at her own pace.

And it worked. While Weasel remained leery of strangers throughout her very long life, she became completely comfortable with Debbie and me, and with the other dogs.

The leave-them-alone approach worked with Weasel just like it has worked with Benji, a dog abandoned at our vet's office who was so scared that he urinated on himself whenever anyone tried to pet him. And with Molly, the Maremma that was considered feral before we got her, and who huddled in a corner of our house when she first came in. And with George, a Brittany mix who hid under the bed for a month when we first got him.

The key is to accept them for what they are, and to make them feel safe and unthreatened. Whatever they do, however they interact, it must be done with them calling the shots. Their comfort is all that is important, and only they can be the judge of their own comfort level.

What makes it difficult is that we almost never have any knowledge about their previous life. So we don't know why they are afraid, what their triggers are, or what comforts them. Forcing or cajoling them might do more harm than good, so we always take the approach that less is more.

The good news is that almost without exception, they are resilient. Eventually their personalities come out, sometimes in a few days, sometimes in a few months. And that is one of the more rewarding aspects of rescue, because it means the conditions have been set to let them live a happy life.

All the dogs taught me . . .

to recognize a beautiful face.

Actually, they taught me to recognize any face, as long as it's hairy.

I have a moderate case of a disease called prosopagnosia, which is also known as "face blindness." Brad Pitt is said to have it as well, so that joins the long list of physical attributes that he and I have in common. In its most severe form, the impaired person cannot even recognize his or her own face in the mirror. I am nowhere near that bad, and the reason I rarely look in a mirror has much more to do with the shape of my body.

It sounds sort of humorous, but it's actually a frustrating and debilitating ailment to have. I am better at recognizing people in context; for example, if I go to my dentist, I'll recognize him because he's in his office. If I saw him on the street,

I probably wouldn't have a clue who he was, unless he was carrying a drill and a syringe full of Novocain.

But the hard part is that when I see someone, I have no idea if I'm supposed to know them. So I don't say hello, even to many people I really do know, and it makes me seem aloof. Of course, in real life I am aloof, but this compounds it and renders it involuntary.

When I worked at Tri-Star Pictures in New York, I used to have to spend a week a month in our L.A. office. Getting on the elevator, I would look to see if anyone else pressed the button for my floor, which would tip me off that I was supposed to know them.

One day I was late arriving for a meeting on a movie called *Band of the Hand*. It was the initial meeting on the project, so it was the first chance for myself and other Tri-Star executives to meet the people involved in the film.

So I entered and there were perhaps fifteen people there. The president of the company saw me come in, and he said, "David, have you met everyone here?"

I usually liked to arrive for meetings early, so that people could come up to me, and not the reverse. That way if I didn't recognize them, it would be easier to conceal.

But in this case, all I could do was reply that I had not met everyone, and I walked over and introduced myself to Michael Mann, the producer, and Paul Michael Glaser, the director. Then I continued down the row and introduced myself to a man that was actually a Tri-Star production executive, and who I had worked with for two years. It was not my finest moment.

Debbie and I met and dated in California, but for our third date, we were both coincidentally going to be in New

York. We were going to dinner, and she said we could meet at the restaurant. I said that if it were okay with her, I'd rather pick her up at her hotel, and she thought I was being chivalrous.

I wasn't. I was afraid that if she got to the restaurant first, I wouldn't recognize her. Failing to recognize the woman on a third date probably wouldn't be seen by her as a plus.

For some reason, dogs are exempt from my inability to recognize faces. We have six black labs in our house, of similar age and size. Anyone would think they look very much like one another, but I have no trouble at all identifying them instantly.

We used to go into shelters where there were hundreds of dogs. We might pick out a dog to rescue that had just come in, and had therefore not finished the five days it had to stay there before becoming available to the public.

So we'd come back when it was available, and would often find that the dogs had been moved into different runs. It didn't matter; Mr. Face Blindness recognized the dog right away, no matter where they had moved it.

With people I try to remember specific things about their appearance as a way to figure out their identity. Perhaps it's the way that they comb their hair, or the shape of their nose or chin. I'm not a visual person at all, so none of it comes easy to me.

But I don't have to do that with dogs. I don't know what it is, or what it says about me, but I get a sense of the individual dog, a feeling, that immediately makes them familiar to me.

I suppose the best way to understand it is that when I first see a person, I see the face. But when I first see a dog, I see the dog.

Rescue dogs taught me . . .

the way out of hot water.

When we were running the Tara Foundation in California, I used to pick up anywhere between five and seven dogs at a time from the local shelters. I loaded them into my shitmobile, which at the time was a Toyota Forerunner.

It is hard to overstate how disgusting this process could sometimes be. The dogs at some of these shelters were sometimes packed four or five in a dog run. That's where they lived, and that's where they went to the bathroom. It's why disease was so rampant there.

So obviously they could often be filthy. The shelter people knew us, so they would hose the dogs down a bit before we left with them. But it was a hosing, not a bath, and they were not exactly springtime fresh and clean.

Then I would load them in the SUV and drive off. We

laid a sheet or blanket down to protect the interior of the car, but the dogs would sometimes get carsick, sometimes have accidents . . . you get the picture. It got rather gamy in there; I drove with the window open a lot.

The net result was that I wanted to spend as little time in the car with them as possible. My preference would have been to beam them back to our vet's office, but the technology wasn't available. So I'd just pile them in and off we'd go.

In such a situation, speed became of the essence. One day on the way to our vet from the Baldwin Park shelter, I was going over the speed limit, and a cop stopped me.

The dogs started barking as soon as I pulled over, and as the cop approached, I had the window open. When he reached me, three of his senses must have told him that something was unusual . . . sight, hearing, and certainly smell. I thought there was a realistic possibility that he wouldn't understand, and might arrest me for animal cruelty. Or a health code violation. Or for violating some kind of mental illness statute, to which I would just plead guilty.

"Are those your dogs?" he asked.

The answer seemed obvious, since they were in my car, but I explained the situation to him. I told him where I got the dogs, and about our status as a rescue organization. I threw in that the dogs were about to be euthanized, since that sometimes gets me the sympathy vote.

He listened to it all, though it had to have been hard to hear over the barking. He seemed to think for a few moments, and then asked, "You got any lab puppies?"

I didn't have any, and I told him so, but I also told him about some adorable puppies that I had just seen at Baldwin Park. He thanked me for the information and for doing the rescue work, then told me to be careful, and sent me on my way without a ticket.

Chalk one up for the dogs.

In the early Andy Carpenter books, I did something called "song talking." Andy and another character, Sam Willis, would play a game that involved working song lyrics into their conversation. It was funnier than I just made it sound.

When you use lyrics like I did, you are supposed to get permission from the song writers, and the publisher took care of that. In one case they dropped the ball, though, and didn't get permission to use a few lines of "You've Got a Friend," by Carole King. They were in a book called *New Tricks*.

One day, at least a year after *New Tricks* was released, the publisher forwarded to me a letter from Carole King's attorney, demanding ten thousand dollars as a penalty for having used the lyrics without permission.

I felt the publisher should have to deal with it, but they felt otherwise. Since I had left them the previous year and taken my future books somewhere else, they weren't really inclined to be helpful. I was on my own.

I called a lawyer friend in the music business, and he said he was sure I would have to pay, but that I should call Ms. King's lawyer and try to negotiate the amount downward. I did that, had a long conversation in which I admitted my error, threw myself on the mercy of the court, and counter-offered five thousand dollars. She said she would relay my offer, but that it was unlikely to be accepted.

My terrific agent, Robin Rue of Writer's House, had been copied on the original e-mail. She took it upon herself, unbeknownst to me, to call the same attorney and express her displeasure with the demand. She went on to say something to the effect of, "How can you take money from this guy? Every dime he makes goes to dog rescue." It was an exaggeration, but unfortunately not by much.

Robin followed that up, again without my being aware of it, by sending the lawyer a link to a video that the publisher had done in support of one of the books. A cameraman had come into our home, and interviewed me, surrounded by our thirty-seven dogs.

Two months then went by after I made my five-thousand-dollar counter-offer, without my hearing a thing. Finally, Ms. King's lawyer called me, with their new demand. They now wanted one thousand dollars instead of ten, and instead of my offered five, and they would donate it to dog rescue.

It was a terrific gesture, and one that I assume Ms. King was aware of. I've read that she is a dog lover, which makes her part of a very large club.

Chalk another one up for the dogs.

By the way, I stopped writing the song talking scenes into the books, and when I tell the Carole King story, people just assume that I've done so for legal reasons. However, that isn't it at all.

When it comes to popular culture, and especially music, I am a dinosaur, with tastes set back in the prehistoric age. Andy and Sam are in their thirties, yet I would have the poor guys song-talking *Westside Story*. I just am always many years behind the musical times; I'm stuck in the fifties and sixties.

When I was in the movie business, I did the marketing on a film called *Blame It on the Night*. It was the story of a rock star meeting and forming a relationship with a son he had never known.

I thought the music was fantastic, and felt we could do an

album, which would be a smash, and which in turn would then guarantee the success of the film. I had no doubt that young people would love the music as much as I did.

To confirm that view, we set up a focus group session with seventeen- and eighteen-year-olds. Other executives and myself were behind a one-way mirror, watching as the moderator played the *Blame It on the Night* music for these kids, so they could say how much they loved it.

The music was so good it was all I could do to not start dancing behind the mirror. Then it stopped, and the first kid was asked what he thought. "If I was a passenger in a car when that was on the radio," he said, "I would ask them to turn it off. If they didn't turn it off, I would jump out of the car." The other comments went downhill from there.

Another tip-off that I may not be on the cutting edge of the music business came about ten years ago when Debbie took me to a Fleetwood Mac concert.

It was that night that I learned that Stevie Nicks was not a guy.

Rescue dogs have taught me . . .

a life can be an open book. *Literally*.

I started writing the Andy Carpenter books in 2002, and the thirteenth in the series, *Who Let the Dog Out?* has just been published. For those of you who have never read any of them, I would say the following:

What the hell is the matter with you? Have you no appreciation of brilliant literature?

Sorry . . . I get emotional about my work. Let me start over:

For those of you who have never read any of them, the main character, Andy Carpenter, narrates the books in the first person, present tense. It is Andy talking, just like this book, as well as *Dogtripping,* is David Rosenfelt talking.

The two voices are very, very similar, and many readers just naturally assume that Andy and I are the same person. I often get e-mails from people mistakenly calling me Andy, and sometimes referring to the character as David. They see us as interchangeable.

My reaction is to acknowledge and understand that they are at least partially correct. Andy and I have some biographical similarities as well as differences; we were both born and raised in Paterson, and lived on the same street. But unlike me, he is a lawyer, and of course much younger and thinner.

But we certainly have the same perspective on life, and the same obnoxiously sarcastic sense of humor. We both love sports, are physical cowards, and have absolutely no understanding of women. There are many more similarities than differences between Andy and me.

I never realized how much like me Andy is until I wrote *Unleashed* and *Dogtripping*, starting the latter as soon as I finished the former. Writing them back to back like that, I realized how identical our voices were, and it actually came as something of a surprise to me. I knew it, but I never really *knew* it, until I wrote those books.

In terms of what readers knew about me, or thought they knew, the fact that they were viewing me through the lens of Andy, a fictional character, provided some distance. They had an understanding of my personality, but not my life. If I were so inclined, I could hide behind the fiction that was Andy.

Then came *Dogtripping*, and there it was; it was all out there. I talked about my life in rescue, but of course that was and is completely connected to the rest of my life. And since Debbie has been an integral part of it every step of the way, she was revealed on those pages as well.

It's a weird feeling, people who I don't know in turn knowing so much about me. Someone will write to me and mention something about Debbie, or even one of our dogs, and I'll do a mental double take. I'll check the e-mail address to see if it's someone I know, and when it isn't, I'm always surprised.

But the strangest parts, and this is where the dogs and rescue come in, are the value judgments people make about us. I assume it comes from my writing immodestly, painting us in a positive light, even amid the self-deprecation.

But because we are rescuing dogs, and it's fair to say that one hundred percent of *Dogtripping*'s readers love dogs, we are put up on this pedestal. I almost never look at people's reviews of my books on Amazon, but *Dogtripping* was the exception, because of my more personal connection to it. There is no doubt that I cared more about reactions to *Dogtripping* than my other books. Here are some excerpts:

"There are a lot of good people in this world, but David and Debbie have got to be among the best."

"Thanks God for people like the Rosenfelts! There will be a special place in heaven for them . . . surrounded by dogs, of course!"

"I am in awe of Debbie and David, they truly have endless compassion for dogs, and have worked hard to give so many in need a better life."

There are many more of those quotes that I could have listed, as well as many e-mails that make the above quotes pale in comparison.

The point is, of course, that it's all a flattering fantasy. If you throw a dart out your window, you'll hit someone who's done more to make the world a better place than I have.

And the other point is that their view of me is, in reality, all about the dogs, and the love that people have for them. If I were a volunteer fireman, meaning if I had real courage and dedication and a willingness to truly sacrifice, and if I wrote about my exploits, I wouldn't get the reactions that I get as a dog lunatic.

But because what I do is to help vulnerable dogs, people react in this way. Dogs are adored by so many, and all I'm doing is basking in their reflected glory.

It's ridiculous, and I love it.

But, of course, the people who praise me are correct. The world really does need more aging, overweight sports degenerates like me.

Every dog has taught me . . .

consistency is what it's all about.

M any people, even very experienced dog owners, will warn that you need to remember that as wonderful as they are, dogs are still animals. You have to be careful, they say, because they are unpredictable.

I find the opposite to be true. Certainly, if I were to approach a strange dog on the street, I could not correctly anticipate what the dog was going to do or how it would behave in any particular situation. I am always cautious until given reason to be otherwise. But our dogs, the ones that have lived in our house, are nothing if not predictable.

Like people, dogs have indelible personalities. In my experience they are thoroughly consistent, reacting almost identically to the same stimuli every time it is presented. I could draw you a picture of where the dogs go in our house every time a FedEx truck pulls up, and I would have everyone in exactly the right position. It's almost like it's a practiced fire drill, and each one goes to where they have been trained to go, and acts like they have been trained to act.

We've had as many as forty-two dogs in our home, and on the rare occasion when a visitor comes in, one of the questions always asked is, "You don't know all their names, do you?"

The question is simultaneously logical and absurd. Of course we know their names; they're our pets.

We had nine volunteers on our five-day RV trip from California to Maine. None of them had met any of our dogs, many of them hadn't even met us.

We had nine dogs in one vehicle, nine in the second, and seven in the third, because the third vehicle was smaller than the other two. So as to be sure we could keep track of all the dogs at all times, we never varied; the dogs in each vehicle stayed in that vehicle for the duration of the trip, as did the humans. We called the roll every time we stopped to make sure every dog was accounted for.

So, for example, the only time the volunteers in vehicle number three saw the dogs in vehicles one and two was when we stopped to walk them, or feed them. Yet by the time we got to Maine, every volunteer knew the name of every dog, whether they were in their vehicle or not. And they basically knew all of their personalities as well. In just a short time, they had all become connected.

Debbie and I have known the personalities and habits of every dog that's been in our house, every bit as well as we know our own.

We knew that Waldo, a black lab who pretty much lay in

one spot in our California living room all day, would start each day at seven in the morning by walking down the hill to the bottom of the property, and then saunter back in time to eat. He would then stand in the kitchen, glaring at me until I served him his breakfast.

We knew that Rudy, a beautiful German shepherd, would listen for duck sounds coming from a sanctuary we had on the property. He would then trudge out there and watch them through the fence for hours, and he would growl at other dogs who came by to find out what the hell the appeal was. They were Rudy's ducks, and he was damn sure not going to share them.

We know that Randy, a black lab, will sit on the recliner chair near the television during the day, but move over to the couch to sleep once Wanda vacates it. And we know that Wanda will vacate it once we go up to sleep, since her favorite thing is being in bed with us. And we know that Molly will get off the bed once Wanda arrives, because she doesn't like sleeping in a crowd, and Wanda's presence by definition creates a crowd.

We know that Gabby and Simon will come flying out to the yard when Debbie or I are hosing it down, yet they have no interest in being hit by the water. They run around, trying to avoid getting wet, though that could have been accomplished by just staying in the house.

I know that when Debbie is out, Bernie is going to camp out at the front window until she gets home. And once she walks in the house, he is going to get so close to her that his large frame threatens to knock her over. When she sits down, he will lay right across her feet. Bernie, if you haven't guessed, likes Debbie a lot.

We know where and when they all like to be petted and scratched, who their friends are, where and what they like to eat, and where they like to sleep. They are creatures of habit, and we know those habits.

I have to admit that I have moments when I worry about whether or not we are giving them the life they deserve. Every one of them gets a lot of attention from us, but we would be deluding ourselves to think that they get doted on as much as if they were in a house with one or two dogs. There simply isn't enough time in the day.

Maybe they're bored; maybe they're not stimulated enough. They seem happy, but maybe they'd be happier getting even more attention on a more exclusive basis.

It's an unanswerable question, and sort of a moot one at that, since the dogs in our house are there because no one else wanted them. But it still bugs me.

Tara and many others taught me . . .

empathy, sympathy . . . dogs have it all.

It takes very little to cause a barking explosion in our house. I am very frequently in my office working, and Debbie might be in the den, or bedroom, or kitchen, or wherever. And at those times, in those rare moments, it is quiet.

But if I get up to go to the refrigerator, and if you've seen my photo you know I go to the refrigerator a lot, they bark. If Debbie moves from one room to another, or gets up, they bark. If one of us calls out to the other, they bark. If the phone rings, they bark. Are you detecting a pattern?

We've taken steps to combat the problem. For example, we often e-mail each other, even though we might be just one room apart. It's just easier, and quieter, though it's possible that some people would say that e-mailing your partner from the next room doesn't really promote intimacy. We're willing to sacrifice intimacy for sanity.

There was a death in Debbie's family last year, and she was understandably very upset. And suddenly, amazingly, there was no barking. We called out to each other . . . nothing. I'd get up . . . nothing. I'm not saying they wouldn't have barked if FedEx pulled up, but the normal, everyday triggers simply did not set them off that day.

And they were remarkably attentive to Debbie. They hovered around her, even more than usual. Bernie snuggled against her, as did Boomer. I know that they understood that she was upset, and they hated to see it. They tried to make her feel better and, in fact, they did.

Debbie and I have been lucky to have enjoyed good health to this point, but we've had isolated physical ailments. She has had a knee surgery, in addition to the recent Achilles tendon and broken ankle issues. I've had a knee surgery and four back surgeries, including spinal fusion.

In all of those cases, we were bedridden for a period of time, and needed a walker or crutches to get around. Try and imagine what it's like to navigate a house with upwards of thirty large dogs, using a walker.

It was always funny when, after surgery, the hospital physical therapist would come around to explain to us how to get around at home. They'd ask questions like, "Do you have stairs? Hardwood floors?"

Well yes, we'd say, we have all that, but we also have something else . . . about twenty six hundred pounds of moving dog. Any suggestions on how to deal with that?

But the truth was that it wasn't that hard to manage, because the moving dogs understood, all twenty-six hundred pounds of them, and they compensated. And when we carefully started moving around ourselves, they basically stayed out of the way and treated us with kid paws. I have no doubt they were protecting us, trying to make a difficult situation easier.

I rescued a collie mix named Annie from the West Valley shelter in the San Fernando Valley. She had a badly broken leg, and a kennel worker protected her as long as she could. When Annie was going to be put down, she took her out and brought her to a vet's office, in an effort to save her.

She didn't have the money for surgery, so the vet just let her languish in the cage, with the leg fracture unset. I have words to describe my feelings about that vet, but I'll just let you imagine what they are. Anyway, the kennel worker begged us to take Annie, and we did. We fixed her leg, and she eventually came home as our dog. She was one of a handful of dogs that we've had that actually preferred me to Debbie. Annie liked Debbie, but she was completely devoted to me.

Our dogs have places within our house that are their special hangouts. It's where they are comfortable, and unless something is going on, that's where they are. Annie loved the recliner chair in the living room; and if I went looking for her, that's where she was nine out of ten times.

With each of my back surgeries, I was in bed for at least two weeks before and two weeks after the operations, sometimes longer. During those weeks Annie was with me twenty-four seven; she gave up her prized living room location to stay on the bed with me, resting her head on my thigh. She was protecting me, caring for me, in the only way that she knew how.

The bedroom, when Debbie is bedridden, is a sight to

behold. We have a large bedroom, and the floor becomes a canine wall-to-wall carpet. They simply will not leave her side. It is certainly true that she has a dog entourage that is ever present, but that is nothing like what it becomes when she is ill, or hurt, or upset.

Of course, football season complicates things for the dogs in their desire to be empathetic. Since I can spend an entire Giants game alternating between cheering and moaning, I'm sure they have enormous trouble trying to decide whether I merit their sympathy, or their congratulations. And when I scream at the television, in ecstasy or agony, they make so much noise that it feels like I am actually at Giants stadium.

Ultimately, it's a two-way street, of course. We are there for them when they need us, and they return the very big favor. Tara was extraordinary at it; it seemed like she absolutely understood our moods and feelings, and reacted to them. And her descendants have followed in her footsteps; she would be proud.

It's another reason that it is so silly for people to praise us as selfless, and laud us for the sacrifices they think we make.

Whatever we give, we obviously get back far more. There are two of us giving, and we're getting back from thirty.

Gabby taught me . . .

there's *always* room for one more.

We've been living with between twenty and forty dogs for almost nineteen years. Put another way, if someone was born when we began this ridiculous lifestyle, he or she would be a sophomore in college. When we started this, there were pay phones on every corner, Dan Marino was playing quarterback for the Dolphins, and no one had heard of Monica Lewinsky.

And for nineteen of the past nineteen years, we've been saying that we want to cut back on the number of dogs in our house.

Actually, I'm the only one that has been consistently saying it. Debbie will occasionally nod in agreement, but she's never been fully behind me in my quest to cut back. I think she's been on my side in principle; it's just that the real world puts up some roadblocks, and very often those roadblocks are shaped like golden retrievers.

If you have two dogs, getting a third is a difficult decision. For example, it increases the expenses, and the barking, and the shedding, by fifty percent. That is a significant consideration.

But if you're living with twenty-seven, and there's a great dog that is going to die if you don't take it in, then you make it twenty-eight. Life with twenty-seven dogs is not appreciably affected by adding another.

So that's what would happen. We would decide that we were through taking them in, and then a shelter would call, and the next thing I knew I had a new dog riding home in the shitmobile. And I'm not going to lie; as much as I wanted to stop doing it, saving a great dog felt terrific, every single time.

But things are different here in Maine; the rescue situation is much, much better. In fact, in my admittedly biased view, everything is better in Maine than it is in California. I'm sorry, that's an exaggeration. California reigns supreme in the time that sporting events begin on television. NFL games starting at 10:00 A.M. is the way to go, and on the back end, I don't have to stay up until one in the morning watching my teams lose.

But in terms of dog rescue, it's no contest. In California there was an unlimited supply of unwanted dogs facing euthanasia, while here in Maine there are far, far fewer. The shelters here have learned who we are, as have rescue groups in nearby states, but the times we are asked to bring in new dogs is far fewer than when we were on the West Coast.

So recently, after our difficult-health winter, I drew the line. No more dogs. We were done. We'd get the number down through attrition, we wouldn't add to it, and in a few years we'd be borderline normal. End of discussion.

Of course, when I draw lines in our house, I draw them in pencil. Debbie, it must be said, has a drawerful of erasers at her disposal, which tends to reduce the effectiveness of my drawn lines.

But this time was different. This time she really seemed to agree with the strategy; it was time to start cutting back. The two dogs that I picked up the day I got sick, Randy and Ralph, were the last we would take in for the foreseeable future. They are great dogs, so we were ending on a high note.

And then a few weeks later we got the call from Carrie, at the Lincoln County Animal Shelter here in Maine. They had this dog that they couldn't place, and they were wondering if we had room. Her name was Gabby.

My first mistake was in asking Carrie to tell me about her, and my second mistake was listening when she did. Because if you called central casting and asked them to send up a dog we could not refuse, it would be Gabby.

First of all, she is a golden retriever, which in and of itself signifies game, set, and match. As I mentioned before, we had made a solemn, posthumous promise to Tara that we would never turn down a golden.

But Gabby didn't stop there. She had cancer, a growth on her leg that was said to be a mast cell tumor, with a potentially dire prognosis. She had just had the tumor removed by the shelter vet, and she was recovering from the surgery. The biopsy hadn't even come back yet.

In addition, she seemed completely sweet, and had another, as yet unidentified condition, which resulted in her having far less hair than a golden should have. Oh, and I forgot to mention, she was a senior. And adorable.

So I picked her up and brought her home, and things did not go well. First of all, we learned that the shelter did not name her Gabby because she was the quiet, reserved type. She pretty much started barking when she walked in the door, and hasn't yet stopped.

But barking we can deal with. Far more serious was that she kept getting into fights, perhaps five or six the first day. She'd go at another dog, and it would seem pretty violent, but no one would get hurt. And as soon as Debbie or I yelled at her, she would stop without us having to physically intervene.

In cases like this, it either gets worse, or it gets better, and there isn't much we can do to dictate the result. All we can really do is be vigilant and make sure that the fights do not result in injury. So we never left her alone with other dogs; when we went out, we would keep her in a room with the door closed.

Things started to get better; the skirmishes became less frequent, and remained easy to break up when they did occur. I was getting very hopeful.

But then came a setback. The surgical incision on Gabby's leg opened up. A lot of skin had been removed in the operation, and there wasn't enough left to heal closed. So we had to quickly take her to our own vet, who was forced to go in and resuture it; it was effectively another surgery.

Once she was stitched up again, there was no way we could bring her home. She would be active here, with the other dogs, and the sutures would likely pop again. Either that, or the other dogs might lick at them, with the same result.

The net result was that she had to board at the vet's office for four weeks, so that it could heal unimpeded, and they could dress the wound daily. When I went to pick her up at the end of that time, I was dreading having to start all over again, reintroducing her to the dogs, and probably dealing with renewed flare-ups. I feared that she would have forgotten the fact that she had been getting used to her surroundings and her new colleagues when she left.

When I got to the vet's office, I had a pleasant surprise. The wound had healed entirely, which I expected, but Gabby also had probably twice as much hair as when I dropped her off. The vet had done blood work and found a thyroid deficiency, which was the cause of the loss of hair. It's very common in goldens. They had put her on a medication called Soloxine, and the change was remarkable.

And when we got home, the good news continued. She had a few spats, but basically resumed the trajectory that she had been on before she left. And today she is, if not the perfect dog, then a damn good one. And her cancer is a thing of the past.

She's a glutton for petting, and one of the smartest dogs we have. She's a worthy addition to the home, which is fitting, because she is the last one we are going to take in.

You heard me.

That's right . . . I'm drawing another line.

My rescue dogs taught me . . .

how to build a career.

I'm a pretty good writer. By this point in the book, you may beg to differ, or you might just differ without begging, but that's okay. Reasonable people can disagree about things like this. My view is that I'm pretty good, at least at writing the kind of stuff I like to read.

But in writing, like other creative fields, such as acting and singing, just being good isn't nearly enough. In some cases it isn't even a prerequisite, but at the very least, talent is a subjective determination.

I've often said that there are worse writers than me making a fortune, and there are much better ones starving to death. Ability is important, but so is getting the breaks, and being in the right place at the right time.

I definitely got big breaks. Some were traditional, like

finding a great agent, and her sending my work to an editor who quickly got my writing. But since then I have had other, less typical breaks. Those breaks bark a lot, and occasionally piss in the house, but without a doubt they lent a helping paw to my writing career when it needed it.

Over the years, many people have suggested that I write about our rescue work and our life with the dogs, but I'd always resisted, feeling that living it was more than enough. *Dogtripping* changed that; I felt like the trip presented a structure in which I could tell the story. And when the reaction to it was so positive, I decided to take one more shot doing it. At the moment, you are reading that one more shot.

But in my mysteries I made Andy Carpenter a rescue person, and I gave him his own golden retriever named Tara. And from the beginning the books were doing okay, getting very good reviews and developing a loyal, albeit modest, following. When I finished the fifth book, *Dead Center,* I felt that I had done as much as I could, and was just going to write one more. Then Andy would go into permanent retirement.

That sixth one, *Play Dead,* for the first time had a dog in it that was integral to the plot, so the publisher put a golden retriever on the cover. The result was that it far outsold any of the previous books, and convinced me to keep writing them. It also insured that there will always be a dog on the cover of the Andy Carpenter books, since many people who e-mailed me openly and sheepishly admitted that the cover was the only reason they bought it.

The publisher didn't have to be convinced. Even before I came up with a concept for the next book, they sent me a mock-up of the book jacket. On it were two dogs, a golden and a Bernese mountain dog. So I actually wrote the book *New Tricks* to the jacket.

I'm not sure that's how Hemingway did it.

So dogs very clearly expanded the audience for my books, but perhaps even more important, they expanded my visibility as an author. And that is a significant distinction. In effect, they gave me a niche without my even seeking one. I have become the "dog guy."

If you don't think that's important, walk into a Barnes and Noble. It is astonishing how many authors there are . . . filling up shelf after shelf after shelf. And many are not represented there, especially in a world where everyone with a computer is self-publishing. Yes, there are quite a few bestsellers, but there are far more writers struggling in relative anonymity.

As a movie marketer, you come to understand that no movie, at least not the ones released by large studios, ever fail because of a lack of awareness. That's because millions are spent to market them; you see so many TV spots that you almost feel like you've seen the movie before it has even opened. So audiences have more than enough information to make a decision on whether to buy a ticket, and they do or they don't.

But it doesn't work that way with books and authors. Except in rare cases, significant marketing dollars simply are not available, and never to the degree that they are for even the smallest movies. There are also many fewer media outlets reviewing books than there used to be, and publicity is very hard to come by. So how does an author get noticed?

In my case, it was through the world of dogs. They have opened avenues for me to reach potential readers that would have been closed off to me as merely a semi-successful writer of thrillers.

For example, there have been many more media opportunities than there might otherwise have been. I've done countless radio and television interviews that focused mainly on my work with dogs, and I have no doubt that it has expanded my audience greatly.

Of course, it doesn't always go exactly as planned. I was scheduled to do a *Fox & Friends* interview for *Dogtripping,* which was to take place outside on their plaza. They asked if I could bring some rescue dogs with me, and I said that I would.

I certainly was not going to drag any of our dogs down from Maine, so I enlisted my daughter-in-law, Amanda, to help. She is very involved in dog rescue, and works with a fantastic group in New York City called Animal Haven. They agreed to bring dogs to the interview.

Also attending the interview was my grandson, Oliver. I should point out that Oliver is tied for first in the rankings for smartest and most adorable child in America (he's tied with his sister, Riley).

So we go out on the plaza, and the three anchors conduct the fairly long interview. Coaxed by a producer, Oliver spent the entire time playing with the cute puppies that Animal Haven supplied for the occasion.

I thought the whole thing went pretty well. I was characteristically informative and witty, and I didn't exhale the entire time, which I have no doubt made me look thinner.

All in all, I was quite pleased, until I checked an e-mail I received fifteen seconds after it ended. A friend was writing to ask, "How come they didn't show you?" And a barrage of similar e-mails soon followed.

It turned out that except for maybe five seconds, the anchors and I were nowhere to be seen. Instead the camera spent the entire time focused on Oliver and the puppies. Fortunately, Amanda recorded the segment, and Oliver loved seeing himself on television when he got home.

Two weeks later I was with Oliver at a family outing, and as I was ready to leave, I picked him up to give him a hug goodbye. "Thank you for being on television with me," I said.

His reply? "You weren't on television."

It was certainly never intended by me, but the dogs have enabled me to tap into a pre-existing subculture out there, that of dog lovers. They have welcomed me, invited me into their communities, and bought my books. They have e-mailed me, spread the word to other dog lovers, and many of them have become my friends.

It's hard to explain the feeling, but I'll give it a shot. Did you ever meet someone who you didn't previously know, but you find out they're from your hometown, or they went to the same school as you did? That simple piece of information connects you, and leads to a conversation based on that connection. You're linked together automatically, even if you lived in different ends of that hometown, or if you both flunked out of the school, five years apart.

No one ever comes up to me and talks about plot structure or character development in my books. Of course, if my books had decent plot structure or character development, that might be a different story.

But instead they come up and talk about their dogs, or my dogs, or dogs in general. They show me photos of them, and ask me to autograph books direct to them. They're comfortable doing that, and I'm comfortable as well, because we love the same thing.

And it definitely is not character development.

Wanda and many others have taught me . . .

that some people treat dogs like furniture,
while dogs treat furniture like shit.

When people wonder why other people treat dogs so poorly, when they reflect on how others could possibly turn a dog into a shelter with a high kill rate, I've always had a ready answer.

It's a different mindset, I say. Those people don't look at dogs as living things, capable of love, fear, loyalty, etc. They view them like they are pieces of furniture, completely disposable, and that's how they treat them. But what I rarely mention is that, when it comes to furniture, dogs have a way of exacting revenge.

When we lived in California, we went shopping for a couch at the Tustin Market Place mall. We hadn't bought furniture in a very long time, because when it's in our house for ten minutes, it looks like it's been there for ten years.

But we really needed a couch; the one we had was no longer recognizable as a couch. It was just a mound of stuff, unable to support human or canine. If I were to sit on it, Debbie would have had to bring in a crane to get me up.

The salesman showed us a leather couch, and then sat down with us so he could make the sale. "Is it sturdy?" Debbie asked.

"Absolutely," he said. "There's nothing you can do to hurt it."

"How about pissing on it?" I wondered, which prompted Debbie to launch into an explanation of our living conditions. Some people, when they hear about our lifestyle, laugh and ask questions. Not this guy; he was there to sell a couch, and he wasn't going to be diverted. He must have been on commission, because he was so intense, I was afraid he was going to try to close the deal by pissing on the couch himself.

He held up a sample of the leather and told us that it would never scratch. I offered him a wager; he could come to our house two weeks after we got the couch. If it was scratched, he'd give us our money back and we'd keep the couch. If it was scratch-free, we'd pay double.

He declined, so I took the piece of leather from him, and made a scratch mark in it with my fingernails. "You were smart not to take the bet," I said, but we took the couch anyway.

Our dogs brutalize our furniture, even though the furniture is always covered. They sleep on it, they stand on it, they roll around on it, they wrestle on it, they chew it, and on more than one occasion a sick dog vomited on it. If the dogs are outside in the rain or snow, they come in and dry themselves

on it. The well-being of our furniture is simply of no conse-
quence to them.

By the time we moved from California to Maine, our furniture, including the "indestructible" couch, was on life support.
Being pragmatic, to say nothing of cheap, I took the position
that we should move it anyway. Why buy new things that
would immediately look like old things?

Debbie took the opposite position, so on one of our pre-
move trips to Maine, we went furniture shopping. We found
a woman named Carolyn Parker who both sells the furniture
and doubles as an interior decorator, and she made the process much easier.

We explained the need for durability, but I don't think
Carolyn really understood what we were saying. People never
really fully get what our house is like until they've personally
experienced it. And at this point, the dogs were still in California finishing off the old furniture.

So we bought four chairs, a dining room table, a sofa, two
dressers, etc. I did record a small triumph; even though our
California coffee table was a wreck, we didn't buy a new one.
We'd ship the old one, which served valiantly as a bed and
place to stand for Wanda and Bernie. On occasion, they would
fit both their bodies on it simultaneously, meaning it was sup-
porting three hundred pounds of dog at once.

I wasn't home the day the stuff was delivered, so I didn't
get to see Debbie put the slipcovers on it. I'm sure it's all beautiful, but as I type this, three years later, I have no idea what
it looks like. It's always covered, and I never seem to be around
when the covers are changed.

Two of the chairs are positioned to the left and right of

the sofa. I suspect that the one on the right must be a complete disaster underneath the slipcover, because that's Jessie's home base. One of Jessie's favorite things to do is dig for rocks, or anything else that might be buried in dirt. The only problem is that in Jessie's case, dirt is not really a requirement.

So Jessie digs on the chair, perhaps hoping to uncover buried chair treasure. He scratches furiously at it, but doesn't seem deterred by the fact that he comes up with nothing, because the next day he is back there digging again.

On a more positive note, the California coffee table keeps on chugging. Wanda and Bernie still nap on it during the day, and Wanda has found a new use for it. When something is going on outside, either a visitor or maybe an animal is spotted, all the dogs run to the front windows and go nuts.

Wanda, apparently feeling the fact that she's twelve feet tall does not give her enough of an advantage, stands on the coffee table so she can see what's happening from a higher altitude. That way she can be well informed as to the goings-on, while remaining literally above the fray.

And it's not just the actual furniture that the dogs focus on. Gabby, for example, excels at a game called "hide the pillow." She takes large pillows off the bed upstairs, brings them downstairs and out onto the property. She then leaves them in various places on the three acres available to her.

She knows she's doing wrong, because she only does it when we're not looking. One time I watched her without her realizing it. When she got to the door, pillow larger than her but securely held in her mouth, I screamed, shocking her and causing her to drop it. I did it that way so she would realize that doing it would get her in trouble.

Apparently I am as intimidating to Gabby as I am to Debbie, because the next day she did it again, and she's been doing it on a regular basis ever since.

What all this means is that if you're ever out shopping for valuable antiques, you're not likely to run into us.

Dogs everywhere have taught me . . .

that they really can make you feel better.

When I was in the hospital, a friend named Rick Skoglund came to visit me. He brought his own friend with him, a huge, gorgeous Leonberger named Jackman.

Rick wasn't there because he's my friend; he was there because Jackman is his therapy dog, and together they stop in to see every patient in the hospital.

Rick is a guy who spends a mind-boggling number of hours volunteering in all kinds of areas. He and I are exactly alike in this regard; the only tiny difference is that he spends all his time doing good and helping others, and I spend my time writing and watching football.

Six in one, half a dozen in the other . . .

I was not feeling great when they arrived, which by definition was probably true of most of the patients in the hospital.

But even I, who was enjoying the respite from the chaos and barking that is all things canine in our house, perked up when I saw Jackman.

There is just something about a dog. . . .

Rick told me that he has been doing these kinds of visits twice a week for years, and he always peeks in the door, explains what he and Jackman are doing, and asks if the patients want them to come in. In all of that time, only three times have patients declined to have them enter.

All Jackman does is stand there, look handsome, smile a lot, and let people pet him, but it makes them feel better. It even made me feel better, and I was sorry when they moved on to the next room.

In case Rick had a desire to be the only one in his household doing great work with canines, he's out of luck. His wife, Martha Kalina, is possibly even more amazing.

A number of years ago she signed on as executive director of the Humane Society of Knox County, and instituted remarkable programs such as free sterilization for cats, and facilitated humane education in local schools. The place thrived under her leadership, and it is a model of its kind today.

But possibly her greatest accomplishment while at Knox was starting a program called K-9 Corrections, in affiliation with the prison located in nearby Warren, Maine. What they do is take dogs that are in need of behavioral training, and therefore unlikely candidates for adoption, and send them for that training at the prison.

Inmates do the training, which proves extraordinarily beneficial for their own rehabilitation as well. It's a win-win; and by all accounts the effects that the dogs have on their human counterparts is extraordinarily positive.

Remarkably, what I have found out over the years is that the dogs don't even have to be present to cheer people up and to help them deal with their troubles. All they need is someone to channel them.

Someone like me.

I started getting the e-mails about eight years ago, and they have been increasing in frequency to the point that it is rare for a couple of weeks to go by without my getting one.

People are writing to tell me about some trouble in their lives, usually health-related, sometimes about a person, and other times about a dog. They are looking for comfort and sensitivity from me, which is certainly a new role I have not auditioned for nor played in the past. Let's put it this way: if you asked friends and members of my family to list my traits, sensitive and comforting would not be high on that list.

Many people tell me that my books, usually *Dogtripping*, have helped them cope with awful things and very difficult times. One woman said that she got her husband to read it during his chemotherapy treatments, and his laughter was such that the nurses came down to find out what was going on. Apparently, laughter is not the norm during chemo.

Another woman told me a similar story about her own chemo. I try to always answer these e-mails, and after I responded to her, she wrote back to thank me for doing so and "talking" to her about it. She said that she'd had the cancer for almost a year, and other than her siblings, I was the only person she told about it.

And then there are the hundreds of e-mails I get from people whose dog has cancer or another life-threatening illness, or who has just died. They are having trouble dealing with the pain, and they write to me because they believe I will understand.

And everybody mentions dogs, which is why they write to me in the first place. We share the dog connection, and my love of dogs gives me a stature in their eyes that I don't deserve. I believe that if there were no dogs in my books, and I were not known as a dog rescuer and as a nut, these people would not be connecting with me.

Of course, not everyone is quite so respectful. I have a good friend from high school named Terry Bresnick. About six years ago, he was facing a parental nightmare. His adult daughter was diagnosed with leukemia and was in the hospital for the bone marrow transplant that could save her.

Spoiler alert: Thankfully, it worked and she's completely fine today.

In one of his e-mails to me while she was in the hospital, he said that she was quite uncomfortable and was having a great deal of difficulty sleeping.

The next morning, he sent me a picture of his daughter, sound asleep in her hospital bed, with one of my books resting open on her chest. He wrote that just reading three pages of my book had bored her to the point that she easily fell asleep. To this day he refers to me as the "Ambien of authors."

I was so glad I could help.

*Our old and infirm dogs have taught
me what is . . .*

the absolute greatest occupation.

I find that when I'm writing an Andy Carpenter book, for virtually every situation that Andy finds himself in, I think of a reference from either *Seinfeld* or *The Godfather*. My view was then confirmed when I read somewhere that Maureen Dowd of the *New York Times* said that in *Seinfeld* and *The Godfather*, one can find the answers to all of life's questions.

So, using the *Seinfeld* reference, I refer you to the episode in which Kramer had a cough, but did not trust medical doctors to deal with it. Instead he found a dog with a similar ailment, and together they went to a veterinarian. To quote the great Cosmo Kramer: "Oh, I'll take a vet over an M.D. any day. They gotta be able to cure a lizard, a chicken, a pig, a frog . . . all on the same day."

Throw in dogs and cats, and Kramer really nailed it.

When we lived in Santa Monica, we used a terrific vet hospital called Bay Cities in nearby Marina del Rey. The owner's name is Dr. Fitzpatrick, and the other vets who worked there, Drs. Brandt and Milo, were equally excellent. We kept our Tara Foundation dogs there, as well as our own.

When Debbie took the job as head of media for Taco Bell, we moved to Orange County, since that's where their corporate offices are located. That left us far from Marina del Rey, so we were going to have to switch vets, a fact that caused us significant concern.

Friends told us about North Tustin Veterinary Clinic, owned by Dr. Kali, so I went to see him. It's an unusual position for a vet to be in; I was there to tell him that we were considering using him to treat our dogs. The net result would be that he was going to have thirty-seven new clients, all of them either old or ill in some fashion.

If you're going to die and come back as a vet, you'd probably want to come back as our vet.

It didn't take long for Dr. Kali to demonstrate that our concern about switching was unwarranted. When it came to being able to get great care for our dogs, moving to Dr. Kali's office didn't cause us to miss a beat.

But then, as we were planning the move to Maine, we got really worried. We had become California vet snobs, and doubted whether we could be satisfied with a Maine practitioner. After all, didn't they spend their time taking care of bear and moose? Or bears and mooses?

So, in the months before moving, we flew to Maine twice to interview vets. We'd make an appointment just to talk, and

I think the vets that we interviewed must have thought we were nuts. But they didn't express any irritation, and answered every question we asked.

Unfortunately, our fears seemed to have been warranted. Like everything else in Maine, the vets were much more laid-back, which doesn't suit our veterinary style. Some had much shorter hours, open two hours in the morning and three in the afternoon. Others didn't take appointments; you just showed up, took your spot in line, and waited until those before you were finished.

We are lucrative clients for a vet, but we're pretty demanding. We expect to be seen when a dog needs to be seen. If it's something elective, that's one thing. But if a dog is sick or in pain, we don't want it to have to wait for care.

So we chose a vet who seemed acceptable, and a week after we arrived here we brought in a golden named Dinah, who was vomiting. The owner of the clinic, who we had interviewed, was not in, and we saw the backup vet. It was not a good experience.

I've spent more time in vets' offices than most vets have, so I have a pretty good layman's understanding of the process. It could be said that I have just enough knowledge to be dangerous.

I certainly know when I'm being bullshitted, and when treatments and diagnostics that are suggested are not necessary. And that's what was happening in this first appointment. But I was willing to reserve judgment, since it was the backup vet, and therefore not the person we'd be dealing with on a regular basis.

A week later, a dog named Snickers had an ear infection. He was rubbing and scratching at it, and was in obvious discomfort. I called the vet's office when they opened in the morning for an appointment, and they said the first opening they had was at 2:30 in the afternoon . . . the next day.

So much for that vet.

I figured I'd have to reassess the entire search, but in the meantime, this ear infection had to be treated immediately. It's an easy ailment for a vet to deal with; they clean out the ear, do a culture to find out what kind of antibiotic will work on it, and then give us the medication. So I found a vet in the phone book in Rockland, about forty-five minutes from our house. The receptionist, Debra Drake, said they were very busy, and asked the problem.

I explained Snickers's situation, and she said, "If he's in pain, bring him in. We'll see him right away."

Music to my ears, and even more important, music to Snickers's ears.

The vet, Dr. Dan Dowling, now at the Camden Veterinary Hospital, is as good as anyone we had in California, and that's really saying something. We've been using him for the last three years, and even though it's an hour and a half drive round-trip, we're not about to stop. He's thoroughly professional and accomplished, and he is supported by two great vet techs, Christine Annis and Sue Luce.

We're in vet heaven.

As a group, veterinarians are amazing. They seem able to do almost everything. Certainly there are vet specialists; our dogs have been to neurologists, surgeons, oncologists, ophthalmologists, and many more. But every general vet that we've had is a walking bunch of specialties.

Take Dr. Dowling. Normal illness? He's the guy. Broken leg? He's the one to set it. Cancerous tumor has to be removed?

That's him. Pancreatitis? Skin allergy? Spaying or neutering? Cushing's disease? Ultrasound necessary? Check . . . check . . . check . . . check . . . check. And he's not just doing it for dogs; he's caring for cats and other animals as well.

And unlike medical doctors, the vets do it all without the benefit of verbal input from the patients. Imagine if you went to the doctor because you were sick, but refused to say a word when asked in what way you didn't feel well, or when you started feeling that way. That might get you thrown out of the office.

In our early days in rescue in California, Debbie saved an adorable sheltie puppy for the foundation. It was not a breed we normally rescued, but Debbie took her because she had what was called swimmer syndrome. Basically it meant that her elbows turned the wrong way, and could not support her.

The shelter was going to put her down, and Debbie had no idea if anything could be done for her, but she figured she'd give it a shot. She rescued her from the shelter and brought her to the best veterinary surgeon in Los Angeles, who basically told her that there was nothing that could be done.

So standing there, holding this sweet little puppy, she started to cry.

The guy never had a chance.

He performed an operation that he had never even attempted before, and actually built elbows for this dog. It didn't just save her life; it gave her a life.

She was never able to run like the other dogs, but six weeks after the surgery she got up and walked with no problem whatsoever. We placed her with a woman from Connecticut, who was visiting family in L.A., and we got letters for years saying how great she was doing.

I didn't mention euthanasia among all these skills that vets need, because that gets into another specialty that they have to master, that of psychologist. We've been around that block many times, so we understand the process and accept it. But Dr. Dowling, and all the other vets, have to deal with people who are completely distraught because the pet they love so much is going to leave them.

He has to talk those people off the ledge, get them to accept the inevitable, and try to ease their pain. Not an easy task.

I know that we've been lucky, and that not every vet is as great as Drs. Dowling, Kali, Fitzpatrick, Brandt, and Milo. And not every vet staffer is as terrific as Chris, Sue, Terry Ryan, Ardell McNay, and Julie Pantoja.

Earlier I mentioned the vet that kept Annie in a cage with a broken leg, not fixing it because the kennel worker didn't have the money to pay for the surgery. Obviously none of this praise is directed at him, or clowns like him.

But we have been extremely fortunate to put our dogs in the hands of outstanding professionals who, in turn, put the welfare of their patients first. It's a major relief.

More troubling to me is the fact that I get my literary inspiration from Cosmo Kramer.

Our rescue dogs have taught me . . .

about some remarkable people in some remarkable situations.

I was in the East Valley shelter one day rescuing a golden retriever, and like I always did, I walked around to see if there were any others that I wanted to load into the car. These were dogs that were going to be placed through our foundation, rather than coming home to live with us.

I saw an absolutely beautiful two-year-old dog that seemed to be a husky, and that was how she was identified on the cage. We hadn't rescued many huskies, so I had no idea whether or not she was a pure breed, but she was a combination of various shades of gray that made her stunning to look at.

What attracted me to her was how scared she was, and when I took her out of the cage and tried to pet her, she urinated. But she seemed sweet, albeit very withdrawn and reserved, and I connected with her, probably because of her vulnerability. I also knew that there was no way she was getting out of that shelter alive unless we took her.

So we did; I got her out of there that day, and took her to the vet where we boarded the rescue dogs. We named her Sherry, and kept her there for three weeks before putting her up for adoption. We did this to try to get her less frightened, and also because she needed to have minor surgery at our vet for removal of a noncancerous growth.

We always used a trainer to work with the dogs, mostly for the purpose of temperament testing them, to determine whether a dog was a candidate to be placed in a home with children. In this case our trainer set out to help Sherry get acclimated to, and comfortable with, her new surroundings.

After the three weeks were up, she told us that Sherry was still very timid, but would benefit from being in a permanent home. She certainly was not dangerous, just unusually submissive. Once we heard that, we put her up for adoption.

I knew that Sherry would be easy to place. Some potential adopters would be turned off by her fearfulness, but others would be attracted to it. They would feel sorry for her and want to make her feel safe. And above all, this was one great-looking dog.

Sure enough, she was adopted on only the second day that she was available. The adopter was a woman, and when she filled out her adoption application, I saw that she listed her occupation as superior court judge in the County of Los Angeles. She seemed to be a great dog person, and was delighted to take Sherry home.

A week later, the judge brought her back to our vet, as had been pre-arranged, to have her sutures from the surgery removed. She asked to talk to me, and her tone made me a little nervous. I didn't know any judges, and I had this image that she was going to revoke my parole, or hold me in contempt, or something.

"Sure," I said. "Is it about Sherry?"

She nodded. "It is."

"Is she not doing well?"

"She's doing fine," she said. "Still scared, but adjusting. But there's something you should know."

"What's that?" I asked.

"She's a wolf."

There are very few things she could have said that would have shocked me as much as that. She had taken Sherry to her vet, who told her straight out that she was in fact not an unusual-looking husky, but actually mostly wolf.

I asked her if she wanted to return Sherry, and she looked at me like I was crazy. She loved her, wouldn't part with her for anything, but thought I should know that what we thought was a dog was actually a wolf.

It was a relief, to say the least. Not only could she have taken us to court, but she *was* court. So I wished her well, and told her to let me know if there was anything we could do for her, and she and her wolf went on their way. I heard from her occasionally, but just to let me know how well Sherry was doing.

We placed about four thousand dogs (and one wolf), which means we met about four thousand adopters. Each one brought their own story, and had their own reasons for adopting.

Debbie got a phone call one day from someone answering our ad in the *Los Angeles Times*. It was from a man telling her that he was not from L.A., but was in fact visiting from out of the country. He wanted to bring a dog home with him, and a relative of his had adopted a dog through us, so he was wondering if we would place dogs that would be taken out of the United States.

"Where do you live?" Debbie asked.

"Thailand."

"Don't you eat dogs in Thailand?" she asked.

He laughed. "Not lately." He went on to explain that he was from Boston, and was head of the United Nations version of the FDA in Asia. He assured Debbie that any dog they adopted would never be on the menu.

He met us down at the vet and adopted a dog from us. Then, when he returned the following year on another visit, he took a second dog so the first one would have a friend. For years he sent us pictures of the dogs playing and relaxing in their Thai home, which looked like a mansion.

We had our share of celebrities that came to us. Charlton Heston adopted a fourteen-year-old chow mix named Willie, to go with the thirteen-year-old chow mix he already had. We also met Minnie Driver, and the creators of *South Park* and *The Book of Mormon*, Trey Parker and Matt Stone, among many others.

One time we rescued a fourteen-year-old Rottweiler named Lulu, and we decided we'd keep her at the vet and try to place her for one week before bringing her home. She was just too old to let her waste precious time sitting in a dog run, waiting to be adopted. Lulu's most distinguishing feature was that she would sit for hours on end, looking up at the sky and howling. Actually, it sounded more like yodeling.

We advertised her in the paper, and the next day we got a call from a woman who lived in Vegas, who simply had to have Lulu. So she drove the four hours to us, fell in love with her, and drove back. They left to go back to Vegas in her convertible, with Lulu sitting in the front seat, looking up at the sky and yodeling up a storm.

If you want to meet some serious dog lovers, run a rescue foundation.

Our dogs taught me . . .

that Green Acres may not be the place for me.

I was born in Paterson, New Jersey. Perhaps you have been there, more likely not. If you have been in Paterson, I can safely say it was not on a hunting trip, or to go camping. If you want to get a sense of what my inner-city high school was like, go see the movie *Lean on Me* with Morgan Freeman. That film is about my school, Paterson Eastside, and was shot there. Our team nickname was the Ghosts, not the Grizzlies.

I went to college at NYU, and did not take courses in agriculture or wilderness studies. None of my classmates drove tractors, or bagged any deer for food. Most of us just went to the cafeteria for dinner, or maybe grabbed a slice of pizza off campus.

I spent most of my adult life living on the Upper West Side in New York City, and then in Santa Monica. You will never see either of those neighborhoods on the National Geographic Channel, nor have they shot any episodes of *Duck Dynasty* there.

So I'm a city guy . . . always have been. Now, there are city people who also do outdoors stuff, who go camping, or climb mountains, or go horseback riding. That's never been me—not even close. My idea of roughing it is having the cable go out, or having a restaurant seat us near the kitchen.

I am also the least handy person in America. When we moved into our house in Orange County, I was confronted with an immediate problem. There was a fireplace in the living room that had propane leading into it. A piece of metal stuck up from the floor near the fireplace, and turning that metal activated the propane.

My concern was that the dogs would accidentally brush up against the metal and turn it at night, when the fireplace was not on. The propane would then flood into the house, filling it with gas and killing us all. These are the kinds of things that worry me.

So what I did was temporarily construct a barricade around the opening with the metal. I took all of our suitcases, and a couple of cartons, and positioned them around the area so the dogs could not get near it. If the Alamo had been fortified that well, Davy Crockett would be selling coonskin caps on QVC today.

And it worked. The barricade saved all of our lives for the three weeks that we had it up. It was a triumph of ingenuity, and I had fulfilled my role as the male protector of the house.

We had a great handyman when we were in Santa Monica, and he agreed to come down to Orange County to do a bunch of things that we needed done in the new house. As soon as he walked in the door, I took him over to the barricade.

I pointed down to the hole with the piece of metal sticking out, and said, "Is there any way you can construct something that protects it from the dogs accidentally knocking into it?"

He looked at it, and then at me, and in retrospect I think he wondered if I was kidding. Then, without saying another word, he reached down, picked up the piece of metal, and put it on the mantel. It was a key, and any time in the previous weeks I could have just lifted it out of the floor.

So that's who I've always been. If something goes wrong, I want to call the super. If I'm hungry, I want to order in Chinese food. If I'm going to the movies, I want to walk there . . . and I want it to be a short walk. I'm not necessarily proud of any of this, but it is what it is.

When we started to accumulate dogs like other people buy socks, we were living in Santa Monica. That happened to be the only city in Southern California that allowed more than three dogs in a household, so we were fine. Our neighbors might characterize it differently; they might use the words "disgusting" and "horrible" instead of "fine," but reasonable people can disagree about things like that.

When we went to Orange County, since no self-respecting city down there would have us, we moved to what is called the "unincorporated area. They only call it that because "uninhabited" isn't technically true. There are some people there, though not many, and there are plenty of animals.

On our first night there, I was lying in bed and listening to these cackling sounds outside, the kind of thing you'd hear from a deranged villain in a horror movie. To my mind, whoever or whatever was cackling was doing so directly to me.

They were saying, "Hah, hah, city boy, you're on our turf now, asshole."

I asked Debbie if she had the slightest idea what was making that noise and, to my amazement, she did. She said, "They're coyotes. They sound like that when they're making a kill."

Oh.

So in Orange County we lived with coyotes, and bobcats, and snakes, and bugs the size of Winnebagos. But compared to Maine, that was like living across from Lincoln Center. Here we have animals of all sizes and shapes, with bugs so large that they call their California brethren "little squirt."

Six weeks after we got here, I felt something on my back when I woke up in the morning. I asked Debbie to look at it, and she said it was a tick.

Stuck to me. Implanted in my skin. A tick. I almost had a stroke, even though she quickly removed it. Literally ten minutes later we got an e-mail from our landscaper saying he wouldn't be at our place that day, because he was in the hospital with Lyme disease. From a tick . . . probably a cousin of the tick that was stuck to me.

I immediately went to the emergency room, and even though they did not see any sign of a problem, I prevailed on them to put me on preventative antibiotics. I was concerned about being sick; but what really horrified me was the idea that that disgusting thing had been in my back.

That nightmarish experience spurred me to action, and we now have a defense against mosquitos and ticks that is awesome. We have two machines, called Mosquito Magnets, operating twenty-four seven all summer. We give all of our dogs Frontline monthly, no small task or expense. But beyond

that, we have a company come out and spray the entire property six times a year.

If there is such a thing as a tick Marine battalion, even
they won't be able to get through.

During hunting season, you see people here in Maine
wearing orange. I don't just mean in the woods, I mean walking on the street. They are not wearing it as a fashion statement, but rather for this reason:

So. They. Won't. Get. Shot.

I don't wear orange, because the only way I would be in
danger of being shot would be during a home invasion. I sit
inside, and when something is wrong Debbie calls plumbers
or electricians or handymen, or whoever.

It's a rough life, but somebody's got to live it.

Some of our greatest dogs taught me . . .

how to deal with failure.

This is not to say that I had no experience with failure in my pre-rescue life. I took a backseat to no one when it came to humiliating defeats, and my dismal track record stretched across decades and subject areas.

Growing up, my brother Mike, three years older than me, was a phenomenal athlete, the kind of guy who could do anything. Baseball was his best sport, and after starting at various levels, he wound up as a collegiate all-star, and set national stolen-base records.

I followed three years behind him through Little League, Babe Ruth League, and high school, and at each stop great things were expected of me because of his accomplishments. Within two weeks, each coach assumed I must have been adopted.

In my sophomore year, I was planning to play high school baseball. I was also sports editor of the school newspaper, and the faculty adviser told me that I could not do both, that I wouldn't have time. So I went to the baseball coach and asked him which I should choose. His response? "You're a really good writer."

Speaking of high school, compared to my success rate with girls, I should have been voted Athlete of the Year four times running.

But it wasn't until I went into movie marketing that I reached the pinnacle of failure. I buried more movies than anyone in the history of Hollywood. And I'm not talking about killing movies made by and with nobodies. Some of the top actors and directors of the era risked having me market their films, and lived to regret it.

Bruce Willis? *Sunset* and *Blind Date.*

Tom Hanks? *Volunteers* and *Every Time We Say Good-bye.*

Meryl Streep? *Still of the Night* and *Ironweed.*

Arnold Schwarzenegger? *Running Man* and *Red Heat.*

Jack Nicholson? *Ironweed* again.

Francis Ford Coppola? *Gardens of Stone.*

Jim Henson and George Lucas? Those two of the three greatest names in the history of family entertainment (Walt Disney is the other) combined to direct and produce *Labyrinth,* which failed under my marketing weight.

Suffice it to say that when I finally left Hollywood, there were no producers, directors, or stars pleading with me to stay.

But failure in rescue is different. It is everywhere, it is constant, and without being too dramatic, it is deadly.

Even when rescue groups are succeeding, they are failing.

When we had a good week and were able to open a dozen spots for dogs that were stuck in shelters, we still literally left thousands behind. If I took one dog from a dog run out of four dogs in the Baldwin Park shelter, I had no illusions as to what would happen to the other three. And that is failure, or at least it felt like it.

If we rescued an eight-year-old dog and he languished for five weeks before we could place him, then that was at least a partial failure. Because for senior dogs, especially large ones, time is precious, and their lives are all too short.

Even some adoptions from a shelter could be considered failures, at least in my mind. We were in the Downey shelter one day to rescue a three-year-old golden retriever, an absolutely beautiful, sweet dog.

The way it works is that on the day the dog becomes available, rescue groups that have expressed interest are automatically in second position, meaning that if a member of the public comes to adopt the dog, they get priority over the rescue group. In theory it makes sense, because the dog would be going to a home, rather than a group, which would then first be trying to find the dog a home.

It only makes sense in theory.

This particular day a guy was there to get the dog, so he was able to adopt it, preventing us from taking it. Debbie spoke to him as the papers were being processed, and he told her that the dog would be in the backyard all the time, behind a fence. In inclement weather there was an area that was covered, so the dog would be protected. He didn't mention how the dog could be protected from the ninety-plus heat that was so prevalent in Southern California.

Debbie gave him five hundred dollars for the dog, who we

therefore named Cash. He wound up with a terrific family in Rolling Hills Estates, an environment well suited to his name.

Rescue is ultimately about reducing the level of failure, but basically it comes down to changing the mindset. I told a story in *Dogtripping* that bears repeating.

Debbie and I attended a meeting when we first started volunteering at the West Los Angeles Animal Shelter. They started the meeting by telling the apocryphal story of a guy walking on a beach where thousands of starfish had washed ashore and would die if not quickly returned to the water.

He started picking up the starfish, one at a time, and tossing them into the water. Another man came up to him and pointed out that with so many thousands of stranded starfish, he was wasting his time and effort. There was no way that one person could make a difference.

The man responded by picking up another starfish and returning it to the water. "I made a difference to that one," he said.

I didn't fully understand it at the time, but they were preparing us for the failure that rescue people were destined to experience. Even though the Los Angeles shelter system was overwhelmed by the sheer volume of abandoned animals, we had to measure success only by saving one animal at a time.

The failure did not end at being unable to rescue all that deserved saving. Sometimes we would rescue dogs that had gotten sick in the shelters and could not be saved.

One time we heard about a golden in the Riverside shelter, sharing a dog run with a black lab mix. Both dogs were said to have kennel cough. It was a shelter I was not familiar with, but I went down there to get them. When I arrived, only the black lab was there; the golden had died from his illness that morning. We named the black lab Bart, and he made it all the way to Maine with us.

I guess the only way to look at it is, like with the starfish, we made a difference to Bart.

Cheyenne taught me today . . .

that it doesn't get any easier.

Cheyenne died today, at around eleven o'clock this morning.

Many people describe what happened as putting her to sleep. I don't use that phrase; she has not gone to sleep, she has died. I often use the phrase she was put down, but that seems a little cold, and doesn't reflect the feeling in the room when it happened. So let's just say that she was euthanized to stop her suffering.

Cheyenne hadn't been eating well for the last couple of days, and had been withdrawn and lethargic. This was a dog with a tremendous appetite, and a craving for human contact. Last night she didn't come up on the bed, which in Cheyenne's case is an earthquake-size change in behavior.

I had a bad feeling about this one. My instincts have

gotten pretty good about this type of thing, and I was worried today when I made the appointment. We've only had Cheyenne for a little over a year, and this is the first time she's been ill. But her demeanor scared me.

We got Cheyenne and Boomer in the summer of 2013, from a rescue group in Utica, New York. They are Great Pyrenees sisters, and were seven years old when they joined our family. They fit in immediately, with no problems at all.

Cheyenne and Boomer both have been sleeping on our bed at night. Because we're lunatics, we frequently characterize our bed dogs according to our assessment of their sleeping ability. We'll call them good sleepers, or great sleepers.

A good sleeper is one who sleeps through the night, doesn't keep getting on and off the bed, doesn't force us to sleep in a scrunched position, and doesn't take up too much space.

A great sleeper is one who provides warmth and comfort, who snuggles up against us, and perhaps lays their head gently on our chest or legs. Boomer is a good sleeper. Cheyenne was one of the greats.

What happened this morning is something I've now lived through countless times. I put Cheyenne on the front seat of my car, because that's where she always liked to sit. I strapped her in, and she just lay there quietly, her energy level very low. She was not stressed or excited to be going somewhere, a sure sign that she was ill.

I talked to her some along the way. I told her that I know she didn't feel well, and that Dr. Dowling would make her feel better. I knew that one way or the other, that would be true.

We went into an examination room as soon as we arrived. Dr. Dowling came in and got down on the floor to examine Cheyenne. He told me that he felt a mass in her chest, but that he needed to take X-rays to make sure. In that instant my worst fears were confirmed. He has said that to me a bunch of times, with a bunch of dogs, and his diagnosis has been proven correct every time.

So they took Cheyenne in the back to take the "pictures," and twenty minutes later Dr. Dowling called me into a different examination room, one that I have been in many times. He turned the lights out and put the X-ray images up on the lighted display to show me what he found.

For some reason, Dr. Dowling considers it necessary to show me X-ray images, even though I have basically no idea what I am looking at. He can take the same X-ray and point to it as evidence of good news, or bad news, and I'd believe either one. So usually I just nod at whatever he's saying, and that's what I did this morning.

As he'd suspected, it was a large, inoperable mass, such that Cheyenne would never again have an acceptable quality of life. I asked him some questions about surgery and chemo, but I was really just going through the motions; I knew what his answer was going to be. It is at times like this that trusting your vet becomes crucially important, and I trust him completely.

Debbie wasn't with me, because she was out of town. She goes to Boston every month for a book club with friends; they read an eclectic group of terrific books from outstanding authors. The next one of mine that they read will be the first.

I called her to tell her what was going on. I wasn't seeking her approval for what was about to happen; I wasn't even looking for her opinion. We've been through this many times, and there was no doubt that she would agree with Dr. Dowling's and my assessment. Quality of life is everything.

I couldn't reach her; her cell phone was either turned off or she was in an area without adequate service. I left word for her to call me, but did not say what was happening. It's not the kind of thing I like to leave as a voice mail message.

I went into the back, and Cheyenne was lying on a blanket. Sue Luce, the vet tech, was already gently petting Cheyenne. The entire staff is incredibly caring to the animals that come through there.

I took my position on the floor near Cheyenne's head, and talked into her ear. I told her that we love her, and how much we appreciate having her in the house. I never speak in the past tense at those times; I'll never tell her what a great life she's had, or how much we've enjoyed having her. On the off chance she can understand me, I don't want her to know that this is the end.

Yes, I'm an idiot.

Dr. Dowling shaved a spot on her leg, found a vein, and administered the pink liquid. I had the annoying lump in my throat, but I handled it reasonably well. Sue and I petted Cheyenne the whole time, including for up to fifteen seconds after Dr. Dowling took the stethoscope, listened for a heartbeat, and then said, "She's gone."

It was an entirely peaceful procedure. Cheyenne wasn't stressed at all. Her body made a couple of movements after it was over, but that was just a postmortem reaction. She did not feel any of it, and now she will never feel ill again.

I don't know much about the ninety percent of Cheyenne's life that she lived before joining our family. I hope she was happy. I do know, without any doubt, that she loved her time at our house, and that it is stupid and unfair that it was cut so short.

I'm dreading the conversation I'll have with Debbie when she calls. She'll be terribly upset, as she always is. She'll tell me to pay extra attention to Boomer, since they have been together their entire lives, and have been inseparable in our home since they arrived. There is no predicting how Boomer is going to react; so far she seems okay, but it's only been an hour since I got home.

When we lose a dog, Debbie and I always drink a toast that night to him or her; that will just have to wait until tomorrow, when she gets back.

The process that we went through today always leaves me feeling wiped out, exhausted. I guess it's an emotional thing; I certainly haven't exerted myself physically.

Fortunately, there are three college football games on tonight, so I'll lose myself in them. I really don't feel like writing any more today; I just wanted to do this one chapter while the feeling was fresh in my mind.

What happened today has happened to us hundreds of times, so I'm used to it.

I'm also damn sick of it.

The rescue dogs have taught me . . .

about the importance of responsibility.

I was married when I had just turned twenty, and my first child was born when I was twenty-three. So I was thrust into a position of responsibility at a very young age, probably long before I was ready to handle it. But I did the best I could, and the rewards were significant.

I think I did okay, at least judging by the way my kids turned out. But I still cringe when I hear the Harry Chapin song "Cats in the Cradle." If you're familiar with the song, and you're a parent, you know exactly what I am referring to.

I've reached an age when my friends have finished shedding themselves of most of their responsibilities, since their kids are grown. I have to admit I wish I could join them in that, but unfortunately "shedding" has a different connotation in my life than in theirs.

Having a dog is a responsibility; having thirty redefines the term. They literally depend on us for survival, and we have to worry about them as if they are our children.

Since we're talking about me, it involves a lot of guilt. The other day Boomer had a badly inflamed ear, and she was rubbing at it, so it clearly bothered her. I saw it and took her to the vet, but of course I wondered if it had been that way for a while, and I should have seen it sooner.

When I see a lump on a dog, my first question to the vet is if it could have appeared quickly, or must it have been there for a long time without me noticing it. I want to feel like we are as attentive to the needs of our group as we would be if we only had one or two, but I don't think we are. I'm not even sure it's possible.

It sounds ridiculous to say, but if we are going out for more than four hours, we get a dog sitter to come stay with them. When we are going out of town, we have three people who set up a schedule and someone is at our house twenty-four seven. It's a hassle, and it's expensive, but we feel responsible. It's like having kids, without the Little League and dance recitals.

Rescue people have an additional entire layer of responsibility. Dogs in shelters are given an impound number to identify them. It's the only way to do it, to give them a cage number would not work because their cages are often changed.

So when in California we might get an e-mail that there is a golden in the Baldwin Park Shelter, impound number A3527680. We would then go to the shelter, ask at the desk where the dog with that impound number is, and then go to that cage. Not a week went by that something exactly like that didn't happen; it was completely commonplace.

So one day Debbie and I went to Baldwin Park, impound

number in hand, to get a beautiful three-year-old golden. We asked at the desk, and they sent us to the cage where the dog with that number was located.

It was an Aussie shepherd mix.

The person who gave us the number had gotten one digit wrong. The golden was there, in a different cage, but it was the Aussie-shepherd mix that had the number we were given.

So we took them both. We felt a responsibility to the dog with the correct number, no matter what breed it was. This is going to sound bizarre, but to not take him because of his breed would have felt racist. And he turned out to be a terrific dog who went to an excellent dog home.

I have no doubt that virtually all rescue people would have reacted as we did. It just felt like the right, and responsible, thing to do.

Where I differ from other rescue people is that I also am stuck with a sense of responsibility to my fictional dogs. The first non–Andy Carpenter thriller that I wrote was called *Don't Tell a Soul*. The hero, a guy named Tim Wallace, winds up wrongly accused of a murder, and has to go on the run.

Unfortunately, I gave him a dog, which means I gave him the responsibility for that dog. He couldn't take him on the run with him, it would have been too unwieldy. So he has to make arrangements for the dog's care before he flees. Not to do so would have horrified every single dog lover that read the book, as well as the author.

It's no accident that every one of my standalone thrillers since then has been dog-free. It's just too much trouble to account for the dog, and it's distracting for the reader. I know if I read a book like that, with a dog, I'm conscious at all times of where the dog is, and how it's being treated.

I make many dumb mistakes in my books, but one of the dumbest was in *Bury the Lead*. Andy takes Tara to a bagel shop, and they sit outside. Andy has a plain bagel and coffee, Tara has water and a raisin bagel.

Raisins are toxic for dogs, and I just simply wasn't thinking when I wrote it. But countless e-mailers pointed out that I had a responsibility to think about those things, and they are absolutely correct. I really blew that one.

That mistake was even worse than when, in *New Tricks*, I wrote that Laurie was shot in the thigh and almost bled to death because the bullet severed her carotid artery. And it was definitely worse than when I wrote in *Airtight* that they found the victim "lying facedown on his back."

Unfortunately, I could go on and on.

But I won't.

Rescue dogs have taught me . . .

all about dignity, and the lack of it.

All dogs, but especially golden retrievers, possess a dignity that is ever present, regardless of their situation. I've seen it when they are ill or in pain, I've seen it when they are out and having fun, and I've seen it when they are about to reach the end of their life.

Scratch a golden retriever on their chest, or above their ass, and they will raise their head, their chin pointing to the sky, as they deign to allow you to do it. They are imperious; the dog acts like the Queen of England.

Now, for all you literal-minded readers out there, I am not saying that I have personally been present when anyone scratched the Queen of England's ass. Nor am I suggesting any of you try it, should you find yourself at Buckingham Palace with the opportunity.

Just take my word for it, okay?

Yet, for all their dignity, the dogs have consistently demonstrated a lack of respect for mine. They have put me in situations that were at best embarrassing, at worst humiliating, and thoroughly degrading. Yet they don't seem to care.

They have forced me to wear an "Eek the Cat" Disneylike suit at a mobile adoption at a Nordstrom, and the pure girth of the costume caused me to knock over four clothing racks, as Debbie and the other volunteers stood there and laughed at me.

They have caused me to literally pick up their shit, without so much as an apology. And then even while I am doing it, they simply squat and deposit more.

I was compelled to wade into our duck pond to save our ducks from a German shepherd named Rudy who had gotten in there. Just to set the stage and demonstrate what it was like, it was a very small pond, we had six ducks, and ducks do not leave the pond to go to the bathroom.

I once pounded four of our dogs with a bag of Starbucks muffins, screaming in a high-pitched voice the entire time, as they attacked an unfortunate squirrel. This was in a public park in Santa Monica, with many people watching. And laughing.

Then we ran six blocks up Wilshire Avenue to a vet's office, with eight dogs and an injured squirrel in a box, with other people watching. And laughing.

I sat on a chair in an open doorway on Halloween so that the kids would not ring the bell and start the dogs barking (they were in the back of the house with Debbie). Not only that, but I "shhhh'd" them when they said "trick or treat" too loudly.

The vet hospital in Marina del Rey where we boarded our rescue dogs was next to a sports bar. On Sundays I would watch guys going into the bar to see NFL games, and they would see me outside, walking dogs and missing those games. It was a complete and utter humiliation; I still have nightmares about it.

I opened the wrong cage at the West L.A. shelter during an adoption day, accidentally releasing a feral and dangerous cat, who proceeded to bite one of my colleagues. The cat then hid, so that the shelter had to be cleared out so that the kennel workers could find it.

I bring the shitmobile in for a detailing every four months, and the last time is an example of what I go through. As it always seems to be, it was a new worker who was assigned to do the detailing. He opened the door, looked in the car, looked at me, looked back in the car, and then looked back at me and said, "What happened?"

I bring three hundred pounds of dog food out of PetSmart on a flatbed, and another customer always sees it and says, "Boy, you must have a big dog." That customer usually has a Pomeranian tucked under her arm.

Everywhere I go I have dog hair on my clothing. I could be standing on line at the bank or post office, and strangers will look at my shirt and ask, "What kind of dog do you have?"

Through all of this I try to maintain my dignity. I fail miserably.

Leo taught me . . .

if you see something you want, go for it.

We were at the all-indoor Seacca shelter one day, choosing dogs to rescue. As I mentioned, it was a harrowing process. We were limited in how many we could take by the amount we had placed in homes that week, and there were always far more deserving dogs than available spaces.

So we would walk up and down the aisles, Debbie, myself, and Ron Edwards, the shelter director. We'd point out the ones we wanted, and Ron would have his people process them out, and give them their shots. It was exhilarating and depressing, in that we were literally saving lives, and just as literally not saving others.

We had reached our quota, and were walking down an aisle of cages, heading for Ron's office to finalize the rescues. Suddenly, we stopped short.

There, in front of us, sitting outside his open cage door, was a five-year-old yellow lab. He had been turned in by an owner who said he was moving and couldn't bring his dog with him. The owner had said that the dog's name was Leo.

He was just sitting there, looking at us and seemingly happy with what he had accomplished in getting out. Ron put him back in the cage and we continued walking to his office.

It usually took about fifteen minutes in Ron's office to finish all the paperwork. It was just the three of us in there, but at the five-minute mark we became a foursome. Leo had somehow managed to get out of his cage again, and he sauntered down the aisle, and joined our meeting. He still had that great big smile on his face.

Leo's message was clear; we were not leaving that shelter without him. There was no doubt we would have to take him, and when we got back to the vet's office we'd figure out where to put him. But Leo was not going to be denied.

Leo's personality made him very appealing, and we placed him in a terrific home in Brentwood within a week. The owner called us about a month later to tell us how great things were going, and how much he loved Leo.

There was only one problem.

Leo kept opening his refrigerator.

Twenty-seven dogs taught me . . .

how to make a terrible situation much, much worse.

In October of 2007, wildfires were raging throughout California, and the state's resources were beyond strapped. Temperatures in Silverado Canyon, where we lived, were in the nineties, and the Santa Ana winds were in full force, bringing gusts of around forty miles per hour, and very low humidity. Perfect fire weather.

Some idiot decided it was the ideal time to set a fire in our area, and he did it in three different places. At first the winds were blowing it away from us, but on the third day it looped around and was heading toward us. All of the houses were put on alert; imminent, mandatory evacuation was a possibility.

Different people prepare for such an eventuality in different ways. We had two other houses on our street, spaced out evenly on a steep hill. Those neighbors got ready by packing their belongings, and then loaded up their cars and waited to see what would happen.

For us, it was a different experience. We had twenty-seven dogs, all of whom were completely dependent on us, and not a clue how to prepare. We couldn't run fire drills to get them to practice getting into the car.

The fire came on us with amazing speed. Debbie had been out renting a large SUV and was driving home. By then the firefighters and police were not letting anyone into the area, and she actually drove through a roadblock in the process. We already had an SUV at home.

If there was an evacuation order, we didn't hear it. We figured out on our own that we had to leave based on the flames being fifty yards away and moving toward us. Our possessions were not an issue; there was no room for them. Debbie packed one small bag of jewelry, and all of the remaining room would be for dogs.

So we loaded twenty-seven large dogs into two SUVs, a process accomplished with amazing speed. Or it least it would have been amazing, had Coki not chosen that time to stroll down on the property. I ran to get her as Debbie loaded dogs, and we were off.

It was a terrible, frightening process, but it was only the beginning. We drove out of the area, and then pulled into a parking lot. We had all these dogs, and nowhere to take them.

So we started making phone calls to all the dog-rescue people we knew, which weren't that many. We were never really involved in the rescue community; we just sort of did our thing. So we didn't have that many people to network.

Debbie made those calls while I started calling hotels,

since we were also going to need a place to stay. And all the hotels were packed, because so many people were displaced. I called at least ten hotels and got nowhere.

Then I got lucky. The Marriott in Irvine had one room, and to their everlasting credit, they were being incredibly accommodating to people forced out of their homes by the fires. They cut their rate in half, and even more important and amazing, they were temporarily rescinding their no-pet rule. They'd let us bring two.

Twenty-five to go.

Debbie reached Ron Edwards, who formerly ran the Seacca shelter in Downey, but had moved to the director position at the Irvine shelter down in Orange County. It is an excellent shelter, one of the best in California. Ron said he could house all of the dogs, and that we should bring them in. So off we went.

This had been a long ordeal, and the dogs were absolutely packed into these two vehicles. Yet no fights broke out, no growling, no problems at all. It was as if they knew this was serious and not a time to screw around.

When we arrived at the shelter, Ron and his staff were waiting for us, and they helped us get the dogs off the vehicles and into the dog runs. Debbie wrote out a list of which dogs were to go in which runs; we tried to keep friends together. No run had more than two dogs in it.

It was a quick process, and within ten minutes, twenty-five dogs were in runs. Louis and Hannah remained in the vehicles; they would be joining us in the hotel.

And then came the moment that turned an awful day into one that was much worse. We always promise our rescue dogs, and I mean a verbal, sincere promise, that they will never have to go back to a shelter. On their first night in our home, just before I go to bed, I tell them not to worry, that they are safe now in their permanent home.

Well, we were violating that pledge; despite our efforts, these dogs were back in a shelter cage. They had no way of knowing that it was temporary, or how long it might last. We didn't even know how long it would last.

It was an awful feeling. We had broken our promise to them; there is no other way to describe it.

They were in there for eight days. During that time we did not visit them, because we feared that if they saw us they would get excited, and might think they were going home. Instead we brought treats for them, which the staff gave out.

When we picked them up the morning of the eighth day, one of the goldens, a twelve-year-old named Barney, was having difficulty walking. When he got home, that persisted, and he also had no interest in food, including the biscuits he had always loved.

I took him to the vet, and the examination revealed that Barney had an inoperable tumor, and would have to be put down. As always, I held him as the euthanasia took place.

It was a low point for me. I'm not dumb enough to think that leaving Barney in that shelter caused him to get cancer, and I'm sure the cancer had been present and growing for far more than eight days.

But I had promised Barney he would never be in a shelter again, and it turned out that he spent his last night in one. It was nobody's fault, except maybe the asshole who set the fire. But I felt absolutely horrible about it.

The fire and subsequent evacuation were upsetting events for us in any case. We were worried about our home and all our possessions, and the fact that we ultimately didn't lose them was a credit to the courageous firefighters who did an amazing job.

But finding a place for the dogs, and then knowing they were alone and scared in that shelter, made it infinitely worse.

Tara . . .

changed our lives forever.

D ebbie, Tara, and I were walking in Santa Monica one day in the spring of 1993. Debbie was working at the FOX network at the time, and was putting in twelve-hour days. I was writing screenplays and TV movies and achieving decent success.

We were talking about our desire to do something more. Debbie felt the need more than I did; for her it was very important. She wanted to do something worthwhile, something well beyond what she was doing. My main goal at the time was to win more than one football bet in a row.

Then Tara got sick, and died, and that was a life-transforming experience. It wasn't even close to being planned; when we started volunteering at that shelter we didn't have the slightest idea what it would lead to. Had anyone told us that our life would wind up the way it did, we would have laughed at them.

It was really just a series of events, neither designed nor foreseen, that led us down the path we took. It has not been easy, and not a day goes by that I don't regret it, but I've never actually regretted it at all.

I'm thankful for so much of it, but for one thing above all:

I'm thankful that Debbie is allergic to cats.